HIGH LIFE

HIGH

Animals of the Alpine World

LIFE

JOHN WINNIE, JR.

NORTHLAND PUBLISHING

The text type and display types were set in Weiss
Composed in the United States of America
Designed by Nancy Rice, Nancy Rice Graphic Design
Cover design by David Jenney
Edited by Susan Tasaki and Stephanie Morrison
Production supervised by Lisa Brownfield

Printed in Hong Kong by South Sea International Press, Ltd.,

HALF-TITLE PAGE: Mountain goats in a blizzard, Glacier National Park, Montana
FRONTISPIECE: Mountain caribou, Jasper National Park, Alberta, Canada
PAGE V: Mountain caribou on cornice, Jasper National Park
PAGE VI: Running wolf, northwest Montana
PAGE IX: Yellow-bellied marmot, Beartooth Plateau, Wyoming
PAGE X: Mountain goat nannies and kids, Glacier National Park, Montana

FIRST IMPRESSION
ISBN 0-87358-634-4
Library of Congress Catalog Card Number 96-6170
Library of Congress Cataloging-in-Publication Data

Winnie, John, 1959-
    High life : animals of the Alpine world / text and photographs by John Winnie, Jr.
        p.   cm.
    Includes bibliographical references (p.   ) and index.
    ISBN 0-87358-634-4
    1. Mountain animals—North America. 2. Mountain animals—North America—
Pictorial works. I. Title.
QL113.W55 1996
599.097—dc20   96-6170

0549/5M/6-96

To my mother.
— *J.W.*

Contents

Species List

THE ROCKPILE COMMUNITY

Columbian ground squirrel *(Spermophilus columbianus)*
Golden-mantled ground squirrel *(Spermophilus lateralis)*
Hoary marmot *(Marmota caligata)*
Yellow-bellied marmot *(Marmota flaviventris)*
Pika *(Ochotona princeps)*
Collared Pika *(Ochotona collaris)**

THE FEATHERED COMMUNITY

American dipper *(Cinclus mexicanus)*
Golden eagle *(Aquila chrysaetos)*
Harlequin duck *(Histrionicus histrionicus)*
White-tailed ptarmigan *(Lagopus leucerous)*

THE HOOFED COMMUNITY

Barren-ground caribou *(Rangifer arcticus)*
Mountain/Woodland caribou *(Rangifer tarandus)*
Mountain goat *(Oreamnus americanus)*
Desert bighorn sheep *(Ovis canadensis nelsoni and mexana)*
Dall's sheep *(Ovis dalli)*
Mountain bighorn sheep *(Ovis canadensis)*
Stone's sheep *(Ovis dalli stonei)*
Siberian snow sheep *(Ovis nivicola)*

THE THREAT FROM BELOW

Coyote *(Canis latrans)*
Grizzly bear *(Ursus arctos)*
Mountain lion *(Felis concolor)*
Long-tail weasel, *(Mustela frenata)*
Wolf *(Canis lupus)*
Wolverine *(Gulo gulo)*

*Sub-species status disputed

Acknowledgments

I would like to thank the following people for
generously providing me with assistance during the
research, writing, and photographing of *High Life*:
The staff and wardens of Jasper National Park,
Alberta, Canada, for their numerous tips, leads and
research assistance; Ben and Cia Gadd for their hos-
pitality and sound advice; Canadian researcher John
Flaa for sharing results from ongoing mountain caribou research; John Ashley, field biologist for Glacier
National Park, Montana, for allowing me access to
his research on harlequin ducks; John Birch, for
providing information on wolf behavior in Denali
National Park; and Paul Menssen and Joel Brann, my
employers, for giving me enough flexibility in my
work schedule to complete this project.

A WORLD
OF ICE

A WORLD OF ICE

There is an ancient world above us. Above the tree line lies a rarefied, bitterly cold realm, scoured by winds and dominated by winter. Amazingly, this is a world of life. Life almost as ancient as the mountains themselves toes the finest of lines between life and death, struggling to survive today as it has for millennia.

Most of the wild creatures inhabiting the high country of North America are products of the Pleistocene epoch, the great Ice Age. They are from a time that seems long-gone, but in reality is still with us—bits and pieces of ancient Pleistocene ecosystems, some complete in almost every way, sit atop our highest mountains, forming today's alpine communities.

Many of the residents of these communities are trapped here by their own physiologies. The physical and behavioral adaptations that allowed them to survive the bitter, icy world of the Pleistocene now inhibit them from living in the much warmer world below. In their quest for warmth, several species sacrificed their ability to dissipate excess heat, while others traded the blazing speed of their flatland ancestors for grace and agility among the cliffs.

To fully appreciate the nature of these high altitude communities and their adaptations, we need to go back in time and look at the era and environment that created them.

The Pleistocene epoch wasn't just a brief stretch of cold weather. Its deep freeze-and-thaw cycles gripped and released the earth over a period of two million years, maybe more. Until recently, geologists divided the Pleistocene into a series of four major Glacial Ages: Nebraskan, Kansan, Illinoian, and Wisconsin, each lasting eighty thousand years or more. Each was followed by extended warm periods, interglacials, of at least fifty thousand years, called the Aftonian, Yarmouth, and Sangamon, respectively.

Under this system, the Pleistocene is officially over and we are now in the warm period immediately following the Wisconsin glacial age, and at the beginning of a new, warmer epoch, the Holocene. Maybe.

Exactly how an ice age begins and where we now sit in relation to future glacial ages has been the subject of considerable controversy. Early theories included one that had our solar system, on its journey through the universe, passing through regions of "cold space." Another speculated that the continents rode undulating currents in the mantle below, and when the continents rose on the crests of these currents, the increase in altitude, combined with increased volcanism (which spewed sun-blocking ash into the atmosphere) initiated cooling that deepened into an ice age.

However, one early theory was based on more than pure conjecture. In the early twentieth century, mathematician and astronomer Milutin Milankovich calculated the changing shape of the earth's orbit around the sun, the changing angle of the earth's axis in relation to its orbital plane, and the wobble of the earth around this axis. Each, when graphed, produced a sine curve. He then took the three separate graphs and drew them along the same time scale. Every so often, the maximal values of these curves occurred at the same time. These peaks represented times when the earth orbited farthest from the sun, the northern hemisphere was tilted more away from the sun, and the spring equinox was latest. The valleys represented just the opposite.

Milankovich theorized that the peaks should be times when the earth's climate is at its coldest and when ice ages occur. This theory did not concur with the best paleontological evidence of the time and was generally rejected by the scientific commu-

OPPOSITE: SASKATCHEWAN GLACIER, BANFF NATIONAL PARK, CANADA

nity. But today, scientists are resurrecting these Milankovich cycles. Advanced core-sampling techniques, combined with radio-isotope dating, are providing an ever-growing body of evidence supporting Milankovich's theory. It now looks as if the Pleistocene epoch may have been made up of dozens of glacial ages and that the old system of partitioning the epoch into four is simply wrong. It is also possible that the Pleistocene is not yet over.

While what is to come is always speculation, many of the events of the past have been established. There is little controversy over the power of the Pleistocene epoch or its shaping of the modern northern landscape and the life scattered across that landscape. Living or inanimate, things that did not bend or change were obliterated. Nothing stood unaltered before the advancing glaciers. In this dra-

matically changing environment, individuals scrambled to survive. Many were not successful—entire genera, even families, fell to the Pleistocene. But there were survivors: tough, resilient individuals that endured to become their species' evolutionary stepping-stone into the future. Even our own ancestors went into the Pleistocene covered with hair and chipping primitive tools from stone, to come out the other end as astronauts.

Beringia

The land was crushed and carved as billions of cubic feet of water from the world's oceans piled up on the northern continents in the form of glaciers and ice fields. Their enormous weight literally sank the continents deeper into the earth's mantle. As the weight on the continents increased, and the weight on the ocean floor decreased, the earth's crust behaved like a massive teeter-totter and the ocean floor rose. This led to the formation of the Bering land bridge, which linked what are now Alaska and Siberia. A broad, rolling plain rather than a narrow span, the bridge and the regions surrounding it formed an entirely new geographic region and ecosystem, an Atlantis risen from the sea: Beringia.

Over tens of thousands of years, Beringia was repeatedly exposed and submerged as continental glaciers formed and receded. Each exposure provided land for restless creatures from both sides to expand their ranges. They didn't just go marching across all at once in some teeming column, but rather, as more and more land was exposed, expanded their ranges by one territory, one individual, one colony, at a time. On their fur and in their intestines they carried germs, seeds and parasites—even organisms that couldn't move on their own made the trip.

Slowly, life reached farther into the unoccupied frontiers of Beringia. After generations, new home

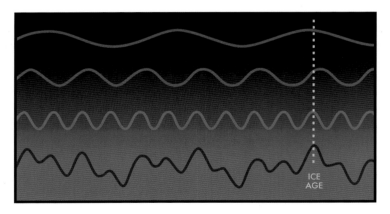

90,000 *Year Cycle—*
Distance from Sun

40,000 *Year Cycle—*
Angle Away from Sun

20,000 *Year Cycle—*
Wobble on Axis

Combined Effect—
Cummulative

ICE
AGE

ACCORDING TO THE MILANKOVICH CYCLES, WHERE MAXIMAL VALUES (PEAKS) OF THREE CONDITIONS OF THE EARTH'S ORBIT MEET (DOTTED LINE), ICE AGES MAY OCCUR.

ranges and territories were established on the opposite continent. No fanfare, no greeting, just a furry creature trying to survive on a new patch of land. And they were all pretty furry and very well suited to the cold, long winters, for Beringia was more than an avenue from one continent to another. It was also a very powerful and effective biological filter that allowed only certain individuals and species to pass. This bio-filter worked in several ways: first, the herbivores had to be able to survive on the plant types that colonized the land out in front of them. Animals incapable of eating these plants faced starvation in what was to them a wasteland. Secondly, only predators capable of catching and killing those herbivores could survive in Beringia. Third, expansion was coming from both directions, and as the waves of plant and animal life met on the plains of Beringia, there were undoubtedly conflicts. Species found themselves facing unfamiliar new diseases, predators and competitors, against which they had no defenses—entire populations were probably annihilated during these crossings. Finally, only the most cold-resistant species and hardy individuals could survive the bitter conditions of Beringia while at the same time reproducing and expanding their ranges. In short, Beringia allowed only the cream of the Pleistocene crop to cross over and begin the colonization of a new continent.

The species that successfully completed the crossing still had to deal with the continuing onslaught of the Ice Age. As the glaciers receded, species expanded their ranges but were then trapped atop high mountains and in large, ice-free regions, called *refugia*, as the glaciers readvanced to cover the land. Isolated, unable to cross the sea of ice surrounding them, individuals and species competed fiercely for limited food and space. These conflicts must have risen to the level of war, and the weapons of this war weren't fangs, or claws, but genes. Competitors survived by using the meager resources more efficiently, by out-scrambling and out-foraging rivals, even by simply

staying warmer. One survived another brutal winter and another did not.

The Mountain Environment

To understand the mountain environment, visualize mountains as islands, perhaps the Hawaiian Islands. In Hawaii, humans have free rein over most of the land above the waterline. Below this line, a different world exists, a world of predators against which we have no defense, of tremendous physical pressure, where even the atmosphere is unbreathable. It is a world of life thousands of feet below, but we are not suited to live there.

At the waterline is an intertidal community. This community is capable of living, at least for brief

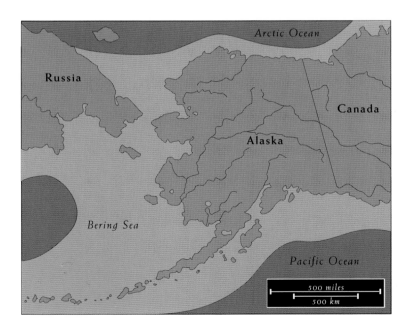

BERINGIA, OR THE BERING LAND BRIDGE, ONCE LINKED ALASKA AND SIBERIA. THE LIGHT BLUE AREA INDICATES LAND THAT WAS ALTERNATELY SUBMERGED AND EXPOSED, DEPENDING ON ICE CONDITIONS.

periods, both in and out of the water. Corals peek above the water and into the air at low tide, crabs scuttle freely back and forth between the two worlds, and turtles make brief appearances on the beach.

Above the waterline, there is a radical change in the environment. The atmosphere is much thinner—a gas instead of a liquid. The weather is less constant, with air temperatures that shift more in an hour than ocean temperatures have in millennia. The winds are faster than any currents. In short, the environment above the waterline is unstable and violent when compared to that beneath the waves.

Mountains on the continents are remarkably similar to islands in the oceans. In fact, mountains *are* islands in a sea of heat and humanity. The waterline, the clear demarcation between two worlds, is the tree line. Below this line, trees grow and the atmosphere

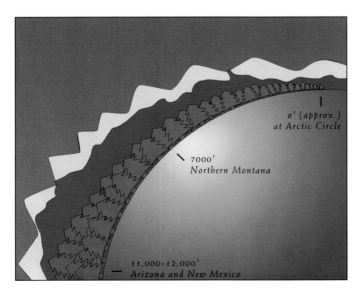

o' (approx.)
at Arctic Circle

7000'
Northern Montana

11,000-12,000'
Arizona and New Mexico

THE TREE LINE DESCENDS IN ELEVATION FROM THE EQUATOR TO THE POLES ACCORDING TO AVAILABLE WARMTH. THE WARMING OF THE EARTH IS CAUSING THE TREE LINE, OVERALL, TO RISE. OPPOSITE: KRUMMHOLZ AT SUNSET ON BEARHAT MOUNTAIN, GLACIER NATIONAL PARK, MONTANA

is dense, warm, and relatively calm. This is the world of forests, grasslands, and all the creatures associated with these environments. Above the tree line, the environment is harsh and the atmosphere is thin, offering little protection from the sun's radiation. Temperatures are low and winter can last over eight months. Winds routinely blow well above hurricane force. This cold, violent world of wind, rock, ice, and tundra sticks up above the warm, calm world of trees, turf, and people just as an island rises out of the warm oceans into the turbulent air above.

The Alpine Tundra

The massive continental glaciers, huge sheets of ice that swept over much of Canada and the northern U.S. during the Pleistocene epoch, are gone. Today, only small alpine glaciers and ice fields remain, scattered along the spines of western mountain ranges. With a few exceptions, these are steadily receding, and as they melt away, alpine tundra plants slowly manage to colonize the newly exposed earth. At the same time, temperate species from lower altitudes are moving up and themselves colonizing the tundra, steadily encroaching upon the alpine world.

As the earth warms, the tree line—the border between the alpine world and the temperate world—slowly rises. Small gnarled trees of many different species, generically called *Krummholz*, are the pioneers from below. They can be seen out alone on the alpine tundra, usually in the lee of a rock or ledge, where their seed maybe fell from the feathers of a resting bird or was deposited by an eddy in the wind. Like pioneers of many species, they are not well suited to their new environment. Lacking the shelter of comrades, sticking straight up into the wind and cold, they suffer high mortality and low

productivity. These trees, usually no more than six feet tall, can be well over two hundred years old and never have gone to seed, their struggle to survive having taken all of their energy.

Around and above the Krummholz, low-lying plants are the rule. Better adapted, they offer little resistance to the high mountain winds, and are covered quickly by the first snows, which insulate them from the bitter cold. Many of these plants contain compounds that behave much like antifreeze, allowing them to carry out photosynthesis at near-freezing temperatures, even below a layer of snow. They also tend to be more resistant to ultraviolet radiation than lowland species, an adaptation that prevents them from being fried by the high-altitude sun in this thin atmosphere.

Most high-country plants are perennials. They have to be, for even with their specialized adaptations, the growing season is so short and the environment so harsh, that they simply do not have the energy to produce seeds every year. Some may take seven years or more to store up enough energy in their roots to take a single shot at flowering. When they do flower, the seeds they produce must be able to survive long enough to take root.

Some plants have taken seed durability to extremes, producing seeds able to survive tremendous lengths of time in a frozen or near-frozen state. For example, a mining engineer in Canada's Yukon Territory discovered an ancient lemming burrow buried in the permafrost. Stored in a neat little pile in the burrow were some seeds, which he collected. He later gave them to the National Museum of Canada where scientists determined they where from the arctic

RIGHT: ARCTIC LUPINE, STONE MOUNTAIN PROVINCIAL PARK, BRITISH COLUMBIA, CANADA
OPPOSITE: ALPINE BUTTERCUP, GLACIER NATIONAL PARK

lupine, a member of the pea family, and about ten thousand years old. They then moistened some of the seeds, and after a few days, the ancient lupine sprouted, grew to maturity, and flowered!

Other tundra plants, such as the glacier lily and alpine buttercup, are sprinters, storing up starches in their roots and then punching rapidly upward through the melting spring snow. In a matter of days, they will have sprouted leaves and will be collecting energy from the sun. This is a bit of a gamble though, as a heavy late spring snow can crush the new growth, forcing the plant back into a state of dormancy from which it may not recover.

Moving up the mountain, colorful lichens, symbiotic colonies of fungi and algae, are spattered across rocks and boulders like impressionist graffiti. The fungus adheres firmly to the rock, forming a complex architecture that encases and surrounds the algae. The byproducts of the algae's photosynthesis, as well as dead algal cells, provide the fungus with the food it needs, the fungus in turn providing the algae with a home. On its own, neither could survive here. The fungus is incapable of photosynthesis and is wholly dependent on organic material for nutrition, and the algae, without the protection the fungus affords, would quickly dry out and die. These paintlike splotches, most no larger in diameter than a tea plate, can be unimaginably old. Bright green map lichens, for example, grow about half an inch in diameter in their first thousand years of life; patches only a little smaller than a dinner plate may have seen the most recent ice-age glaciers recede. Others, such as the bright red jewel lichens, are dependent on animal waste for fertilizer: their bright colonies mark frequently used animal perches.

LEFT: GLACIER LILIES, GLACIER NATIONAL PARK AND NORTHWEST MONTANA
OPPOSITE: MOSS CAMPION, GLACIER NATIONAL PARK

At the upper limit of the tundra, where bare rock is the rule, circular cushions of low-lying moss campion dot the bleak landscape. A pioneer of the alpine plant world, it can grow where there is virtually no soil, anchoring itself with hairlike roots directly to rock. If there is a suitable crack in the rock's surface, the plant will send a taproot deep below. Its dense green cushion provides a home for other plants, and as the cushion slowly expands, a small alpine community, a piece of tundra, is formed. This is a painfully slow process, for the moss campion disk grows about an inch in diameter every five years; it may be ten or more years old before it blooms, showing the world its tiny purple flowers. At best, the moss campion's grip on the mountain is tenuous, relying more on aerodynamics than root strength to keep it anchored against howling winds; if it is poked or prodded, the entire plant is easily dislodged.

This world of low-lying plants, snow, rock, and wind is occupied by a select group of animals. They are tough, ice-age relics and superbly suited to these soaring heights. The nature of their lives and the adaptations that allow them to survive on their lofty islands are the subjects of this story.

LEFT: LICHENS, GLACIER NATIONAL PARK
OPPOSITE: MOSS CAMPION, GLACIER NATIONAL PARK

YELLOW-BELLIED MARMOT, BEARTOOTH PLATEAU, WYOMING

THE
ROCKPILE
COMMUNITY

THE ROCKPILE COMMUNITY

The sun breaks over the ridge, its light spilling over and filling the cirque—a steep-walled concave basin—beyond. Along with the visible light comes invisible infrared radiation, heat, and the basin quickly warms. Soon, the talus slope, a boulder field below a crumbling cliff, begins to steam as the thin layer of frost on the rocks melts, then evaporates—the steaming boulders seem to move, a glistening, misty river. An echoing clatter breaks the silence as a small piece of the cliff loses its grip and tumbles down, bouncing off the boulders below. A grizzled gray rock comes to life and raises its head to watch the ricocheting, noisy intruder. Soon this "rock" is joined by others, and hoary marmots, rousted from their morning sunbathing by the rockfall, waddle among the boulders. Some leave the talus to feed out on the adjoining tundra; others engage in playful wrestling matches.

More shapes move among the rocks. A tiny pika, lightning fast, zips by with a mouthful of grasses and disappears under a dark overhang. Twenty feet away, it reemerges empty-mouthed, climbs to the top of a small boulder, and emits a loud, nasal, "eek!". Then, as if scared by the sound of its own voice, it quickly backs away from the top of the boulder and hunkers down. Another "eek!" echoes faintly from another pile of rocks out in the cirque. The pika ignores the response and disappears, a tan blur.

Along the edge of the talus, a golden-mantled ground squirrel moves quickly and purposefully from one patch of vegetation to the next, gleaning select bits of leaves, blossoms, and seeds and storing them in cheek pouches to eat later in the protection of the rocks. Out from the talus, Columbian ground squirrels stand upright at the mouths of their burrows, chirping territorial proclamations. Occasionally, rival males engage in bounding, squeaking, high-speed chases among the rocks and across the tundra. Everywhere in and around the talus slope, furry critters are feeding, scurrying, calling, or napping.

Talus slopes throughout the mountains support highly structured animal communities. Despite the apparent free-for-all, each species within the community operates with its own well-defined social order. The mix of species in these communities—from the Colorado Rockies all the way up to the Alaska Range—is

I'D ALWAYS ASSUMED THAT MARMOTS WHISTLED BY BLOWING AIR THROUGH THOSE BIG SQUARED-OFF BUCK TEETH. I LEARNED OTHERWISE ONE AFTERNOON WHEN I WAS PHOTOGRAPHING THE DOMINANT MALE OF MY FAVORITE TALUS SLOPE. HE WAS SPRAWLED OUT, SUNNING HIMSELF ON HIS USUAL BOULDER. I WAS ABOUT TWENTY FEET DOWNSLOPE, HAD JUST FINISHED OFF A ROLL OF FILM, AND WAS RELOADING MY CAMERA WHEN HE SAT UP AND OPENED HIS MOUTH AS IF TO YAWN.

GAPING RIGHT AT ME, HE LET OUT A SONIC BLAST THAT I ACTUALLY FELT STRIKE MY FACE. MY EARS WERE RINGING AS I FUMBLED WITH LOADING A NEW ROLL OF FILM INTO THE CAMERA. HE CONTINUED TO WHISTLE, TURNING TO SEND BLAST AFTER BLAST IN ALL DIRECTIONS. WHEN HE FINISHED, HE CASUALLY STRETCHED BACK OUT AND RESUMED SUNNING HIMSELF. I WAS ALL BUT DEAF.

ON ANOTHER OCCASION, I SAW TWO GOLDEN EAGLES THAT HAD A MARMOT TRAPPED UNDER A ROCK. ONE EAGLE WAS WALKING AROUND ON THE GROUND TRYING TO FLUSH THE MARMOT FROM UNDER THE BOULDER, WHILE THE OTHER WAS PERCHED NEARBY, READY TO POUNCE THE SECOND HE MADE A RUN FOR IT. THE MARMOT LET OUT BLAST AFTER BLAST AND THESE SEEMED TO ACTUALLY REPEL THE EAGLE ON THE GROUND.

OPPOSITE: HOARY MARMOT WHISTLING, GLACIER NATIONAL PARK

remarkably similar. Marmots, pika, and a few representatives of the local species of ground squirrel inhabit many of the high country's talus slopes.

Marmot

Marmots are generally believed to have originated in the mountains of central Asia early in the Pleistocene. From there they radiated outward, colonizing virtually all of Eurasia in one form or another. Eventually they reached Siberia, crossed Beringia, and colonized most of northern North America. Their ability to expand their range so dramatically is not due to any talent for walking great distances, for marmots rarely move more than a half-mile from where they were born. Rather, it is a reflection of the amount of time that they have had as a genus. Even at an expansion rate of only a half-mile a year, marmota have existed long enough to circle the earth several times.

In North America, marmots have colonized most of the continental U.S. and Canada. In the lowlands of the eastern U.S. and throughout most of Canada's southern provinces, the local marmot is the woodchuck. In the mountains of the West, depending on which scientist you're talking to, there are two to four different species of marmot: hoary, yellow-bellied, Olympic, and Vancouver. In scientific circles, the argument is over whether the Olympic marmot, found on Washington's Olympic peninsula, and the Vancouver marmot, found on Canada's Vancouver Island, are truly separate species, or are actually the same species as hoaries. Recent genetic and behavioral comparisons by Russian, American, and Canadian researchers seem to indicate the latter.

The Russians found that our hoary, Olympic, and

HOARY MARMOTS PLAYING, GLACIER NATIONAL PARK

Vancouver marmots are almost genetically indistinguishable from one another—they're all basically hoaries. Russian researchers also found that hoaries are very closely related to the Siberian black-capped marmot, suggesting that at the least, they shared a common ancestor. The pioneer marmot species that made the first Beringia crossing probably looked a lot like the black-capped and hoary marmots of today.

The exclusively alpine hoary marmot is pretty hard not to like. The largest member of the squirrel family, these twenty-pound, grizzle-furred rodents beg, perform, or rustle their way into the hearts of many high-country travelers. The hoary's curiosity makes it the bane of researchers trying to study other talus inhabitants, as marmots will methodically investigate and then dismantle every measuring instrument or live trap set in "their" rockpile.

Hoaries are social animals. Each colony is essentially one big family, with a dominant male, one to six reproductive-age females, and the young from the current as well as previous two years. A transient male can sometimes be found hovering on the perimeter. The particular talus slope he dominates determines whether or not the dominant male is monogamous or has a harem. If the rocks are surrounded by ample vegetation, more than one female will move in. A meager supply usually dictates that only one female will take up residence and that she will be very aggressive toward any other females that show up.

Each colony has several burrows, their entrances usually under boulders or overhangs. Each of these burrows has a specific purpose. Females breed every other year, and those with young commandeer private burrows from which they exclude all other members of the colony. Near the physical center of the colony will be one to three large, deep burrows ending in sizable chambers. These will be shared throughout the summer by the dominant male, non-breeding females, and any yearlings still with the group. Out near the edge of the colony, where the rocks end and vegetation begins, there are usually a couple of shallow burrows just inside the perimeter that are used as emergency escape shelters in case a predator shows up during a feeding foray.

Some marmot pairs are tremendously affectionate with each other and their young. Even in non-breeding years, these couples spend time in close physical contact, either snuggled up together in the sun on their favorite boulder or grooming each other. In the years when they have young, the whole family may spend hours feeding and playing together morning after morning.

The hoary's long, piercing whistle is a familiar sound in the high country. The sound is strong and clear, even when it originates from more than a mile away. As much a part of the high country as wind and snow, this sound has earned them the nickname "whistler." Hoaries whistle for a variety of reasons, most often as an alarm call. The shrill sound almost always means a predator has been spotted, usually a golden eagle, and the warning calls are passed from colony to colony, a surreal echoing chain down a mountain ridge. Another whistled signal is a simple territorial proclamation: "I'm here, don't mess with my rockpile!"

It's possible that the marmot's whistle is used for more than communication; it may also serve as a form of sonic defense. Since hoaries live almost exclusively in and around talus slopes, they are vulnerable to entrapment under boulders by predators. Many predators have very sensitive hearing, and the marmot's painfully high-pitched whistle could force the predator to break off its attack.

In addition to whistling, there is something else that hoaries do exceedingly well: sleep. The ultimate power-loungers, marmots spend over eighty percent of their lives either asleep or in a state of hibernation.

Put another way, a twelve-year-old hoary has been awake and alert for about two years and asleep or dormant for nearly ten. Each year, usually in mid- to late September, all the members of a colony descend together into one or two hibernation burrows, or *hibernacula*. There, piled in large furry bundles, they slip into a state of dormancy so deep that signs of life are almost undetectable. Their body temperatures fall to under forty degrees Fahrenheit and their heart and respiration rates slow to one beat and breath every three to six minutes. During this period, they live solely on their fat reserves, losing about forty percent of their total body weight before spring's arrival. No food stash, no water, no evacuation: just the slow consumption of their own bodily resources. They remain in this state for about nine months. Awakening in mid- to late June, they emerge into another high-country spring; perhaps to them, there is no winter, just one long springtime, interrupted by naps.

Yellow-bellied marmots are found from the Rockies in northern New Mexico, west to the California Sierra, and north to the valleys of central British Columbia. Unlike hoaries, yellow-bellied marmots are not exclusively alpine. They can be found at alpine elevations, usually above eight thousand feet, only at the southern end of their range. The species loses altitude as it moves north, until, at the far northern end of their range, they are valley dwellers. Their range overlaps with that of the hoary marmot throughout the Montana Rockies and the Sawtooth and Bitterroot mountains of Idaho, but yellow-bellies are always found at lower elevations.

Avoidance of direct competition with hoaries may account for this. Yellow-bellies top out at around ten pounds, about half the weight of a hoary, and wouldn't stand a chance in a dispute over rockpile ownership. Climatic adaptations probably play the largest role in the distribution of the two species, however. Hoaries

have denser coats and larger fat reserves than yellow-bellies, which means that they cannot easily dissipate excess internal heat. They wouldn't be able to live in the high temperatures that are common at lower elevations and to the south. Yellow-bellies, on the other hand, forage in heat with little problem. The trade-off is that being a better heat-dissipater means that the yellow-belly is a poor heat-conserver; where the weather is cold and the winter long, this is a major handicap. Yellow-bellies can manage only about seven months of hibernation before their reserves are depleted. Over an extended winter, the mortality rate can top eighty percent in a yellow-belly colony.

There are social differences between the two species as well. Where about fifty percent of hoaries are monogamous, yellow-bellies are virtually always polygamous, sometimes extraordinarily so. Adult male-to-female ratios in a yellow-belly colony are as high as one to eighteen. Males vigorously defend their harems against interlopers and are very intolerant of even their own male offspring. It's rare that the young of either sex stay in the colony for more than a year, due to ever-increasing aggression from the parents. Competition between females within a harem can also take a rather grim turn; females will often kill, and sometimes eat, each other's offspring. As a result, birthing burrows are fiercely defended. Overall, yellow-belly colonies tend to be less stable and peaceful than hoary colonies—rough-and-tumble Old West towns rather than 1950s suburban America.

Yellow-bellied marmot, Beartooth Plateau

Pika

Despite their looks, Pika aren't related to the chinchilla or guinea pig. These six-ounce, mitten-sized creatures are actually North America's smallest members of the rabbit order, Lagomorpha. They can be found from northern New Mexico and central California to Alaska, Yukon, and the Northwest Territory. Pika live at low elevations at the extreme northern end of their range, which is near the Arctic Circle, whereas at the southern end of their range, they are exclusively mountain dwellers. Here, they rarely venture more than a few hundred feet below tree line.

It's hard to imagine an animal as cute and fuzzy as the pika to be particularly fierce and territorial. But these guys are. Males and females alike stake out territories within a talus slope and defend them with a passion that would do a lion proud. Each little territory is fifty to one hundred feet across and usually borders on a patch of vegetation. The biggest territories, bordering the most vegetation, are owned by the biggest, most aggressive individuals. Pika mark their territories with scent from a cheek gland and routinely call from rock perches. If these warnings fail to keep out a trespasser, they will do battle.

The only time pika let up on territorial defense is during the brief mating season early in the spring. As a female enters estrus, she leaves her own territory in search of a nearby male. She enters his territory and after a short courtship, the pair mates. In a nest tucked away under the rocks and made from local vegetation, the female delivers a litter of two to five after an approximate thirty-day gestation. As the offspring get older, even before they are weaned, all of the members of the pika family display ever-increasing aggression toward each other. Fortunately, young pika mature quickly; in only a month they are fully weaned and on their own. They are then quickly forced out of the male's territory, and the female returns to her own territory, evicting any squatters that may have moved in during her absence.

This is a very hard time for the year's young. They are at the bottom of the totem pole, inexperienced, and on the receiving end of constant assaults as they wander through the established territories of adults. Their mortality probably exceeds fifty percent in the first month after weaning, and those who do not find a vacant territory by autumn will almost certainly die before the first snows. Aggression seems to be the

I ONCE WITNESSED A BATTLE THAT RESULTED IN A SMALL TERRITORY BEING ANNEXED BY A DOMINANT NEIGHBOR. I WAS PHOTOGRAPHING A VERY "CLEAN", SCAR-FREE PIKA WHEN ANOTHER PIKA, ABOUT FIFTY FEET AWAY, LET OUT A GOOD, SOLID, "EEK!" MY PIKA IMMEDIATELY RESPONDED WITH HIS OWN CALL, AND "EEKING" ALL THE WAY, THE TWO APPROACHED EACH OTHER THROUGH THE ROCKS. SOON, THEY WERE FIVE FEET APART, EACH ON A ROCK, EACH FURIOUSLY SQUEAKING. EVEN FROM FIFTY FEET, I COULD TELL MY PIKA DIDN'T HAVE A PRAYER, AND I THINK HE KNEW IT TOO.

THE INTRUDER WASN'T NOTICEABLY BIGGER, BUT HE HAD THE MOST SCARRED-UP COAT I'VE EVER SEEN. NEXT TO THIS CRUSTY WARRIOR, MY PIKA LOOKED LIKE SOME KIND OF DUDED-UP DANDY. THE WARRIOR CHARGED, THE DANDY HELD HIS GROUND, AND THE TWO TUMBLED IN A SQUEAKING, FURRY MASS, DOWN INTO THE BOULDERS. WATCHING THEM GO AT IT WAS LIKE SEEING A MOVIE RUN AT THREE TIMES NORMAL SPEED. IN A MATTER OF SECONDS, THE FIGHT HAD CROSSED THIRTY FEET OF TALUS. THE DANDY WENT SQUIRTING OUT OF THE ROCKS AND OFF ACROSS THE TUNDRA WHILE THE WARRIOR SPENT THE NEXT SEVERAL MINUTES RUNNING FROM ROCK TO ROCK CALLING, PROCLAIMING HIS NEW OWNERSHIP OF THE TALUS.

OPPOSITE: PIKA, BEARTOOTH PLATEAU

key to their survival. Only those young capable of finding and then holding onto a territory have a chance of surviving their first winter.

Evolution has almost totally eliminated the pika's capacity to dissipate excess heat. Rabbit-like features such as long legs, big feet, big ears, a long nose, or a tail help regulate internal temperature but would be a distinct disadvantage in the extreme cold of high country. So, unlike their cousins, pika have very small feet and ears, short legs, no visible tail, and no nose to speak of. Their heat retention is so effective that exposure to ninety degrees Fahrenheit in the shade for as little as an hour can be fatal to them.

These adaptations also mean that southern pika are stranded right on the tops of many mountains, unable to venture down to interconnecting ridges because of the heat. This is a potentially serious problem—there is only limited room near the tops of mountains and some of these small, isolated communities have become seriously inbred. In some populations, all of the individuals are more closely related than a normal pika parent is to its own offspring. Inbreeding on this scale results in tremendous vulnerability to all kinds of natural disasters. In most healthy, genetically diverse populations, there will be at least a few individuals capable, through some unique genetic combination, of surviving most crises. In populations with little genetic variety, chances are that if a serious epidemic or other disaster occurs, every single member of the population will succumb.

Despite their cold-weather adaptations, northern pika suffer the metabolic dilemma common to all small animals: staying warm through the long winter. The problem is one of size, which can be illustrated with some simple math. Suppose you're a cube-shaped creature, one inch long on each side. Your internal volume, your furnace, would be one cubic

PIKA, BEARTOOTH PLATEAU

inch. Your outer surface, your skin, which dissipates heat, would be six square inches (the six sides of the cube). This gives you a ratio of one to six, furnace-to-surface area.

Now do the same equation with a cube ten inches on each side. The interior, the furnace, is one thousand cubic inches and the surface skin is six hundred square inches. This gives you a ratio of ten to six (one thousand to six hundred), furnace-to-surface area. The ratio of heater to surface area jumps from one to six all the way up to ten to six just by getting bigger. Basically, what this means is that if you're big, you use fewer of your calories to maintain your body temperature, and if you're small, you use most of your calories just to stay warm.

Pika, being small creatures, have to eat constantly to survive in their environment. This doesn't pose much of a challenge in the spring and summer when there's plenty of fresh vegetation, but in the winter, with little natural food around, it becomes much more difficult. Unlike animals that escape winter through hibernation, pika face it head-on. They do this by stockpiling huge stashes of dried vegetation, "hay piles," throughout their territory. In about mid-July, pika begin leaving small piles of vegetation lying about on rocks, drying in the sun. Once a smaller pile has dried, they haul it off to a big, central pile, usually under an overhang. There are generally several of these hay piles within a pika's territory, and as the piles grow, so does the pika's aggression. These hay piles are life and death to the animal and represent a huge investment in time and energy—without them, the pika cannot outlast the winter. The hay piles alone may not be all that keeps the animals alive. Like other members of the rabbit order, pika may be able to reingest their own droppings (animals that can do this are called *coprophages*), squeezing every last bit of nutrition out of their food supplies. For seven to nine months, the pika's talus-slope terri-

tory will be buried under snow and ice. Down there in the dark, little pika wars are probably fought over space and precious hay piles.

Each spring, when the snow releases the talus, a handful of battered survivors climbs up out of the darkness and into the sun, proclaiming their victory over winter: "Eek!"

Ground Squirrels

Two species of ground squirrel are commonly found scurrying around alpine tundra and meadows, often along the fringes of talus slopes. The golden-mantled ground squirrel ranges from northern New Mexico west to the Sierra, and northward to central Alberta and British Columbia. The Columbian ground squirrel is found from Montana and central Idaho, west into eastern Oregon and Washington, to about as far north as its golden-mantled cousin.

Both species have broad tastes in making a home. You are likely to find Columbians wherever there are open spaces and fresh vegetation, whether it's in a rancher's valley pasture or a high mountain meadow just above tree line. Golden-mantleds are also found over a wide range of habitats, although they tend to stick to more broken, rocky terrain than Columbians and can be found at much higher altitudes, even on the highest wind-swept ridges.

Both species are small. Columbians rarely top a pound, and golden-mantleds only reach about ten ounces; both are approximately the same length, eight to twelve inches. With their greater weight, Columbians are noticeably beefier-looking—overall, they have a chubby, marmot-like appearance, while golden-mantleds look more like overgrown chipmunks, for which they are often mistaken due to the twin stripes that decorate each flank.

In some areas, golden-mantleds take over old

Columbian burrows to use as dens and nesting chambers; they are, however, capable of doing their own excavation. Stashes of food in tunnel entrances and in underground chambers led some early naturalists to think that these two species were active year-round, living on subterranean food stores through the winter. They don't. The food reserves were actually either nesting material or small caches for a rainy (or extremely hot) day. Typical of almost all ground squirrels, both species are hibernators, spending at least half of each year in a state of dormancy deep in a burrow. Columbians typically go into hibernation by mid-August at lower elevations, and by early to mid-September at high altitudes. The difference is probably due to the more plentiful food supplies that allow the low-altitude squirrels to gain weight faster and go into hibernation earlier.

When they head underground, Columbians seal themselves in with earthen plugs that measure from two to six feet long; oxygen diffusing through the soil sustains them through hibernation. Once they've gone under, Columbians' breathing and heart rates fall to a slow, steady one every four minutes, and their body temperature falls to approximately forty degrees Fahrenheit. After a seven-month dormancy, they emerge whether spring has arrived or not. On their way out, they burrow straight up through the earth rather than following the original tunnel.

Golden-mantleds usually begin hibernation in mid-October and also have a seven-month dormancy. Their style of hibernation is a little different from Columbians and marmots in that, instead of descending into a deeply torpid state and staying there, golden-mantleds appear to cycle between life and death. For up to six minutes, this small creature does not breathe, nor does its heart beat. Then, suddenly,

it comes to life with a series of rapid, shallow breaths and heartbeats. Just as suddenly, these stop and for several more minutes there are no signs of life.

Columbians usually form colonies, some extremely large. At lower elevations with lots of continuous habitat, these colonies can contain hundreds, even thousands of individuals. When their numbers get this high, particularly in an agricultural area, they can do serious crop and pasture damage. Needless to say, many local ranchers and farmers view them as pests and Columbians are gassed in their burrows and shot and poisoned by the thousands throughout their range. Yet they manage to survive and even thrive. Ironically, humans' ever-increasing agricultural and ranching activity provides Columbians with more and more clearings to colonize, keeping their numbers high despite constant attacks.

In the mountains, where habitat is broken and food limited by the short growing season, Columbians form considerably smaller colonies that very closely resemble those of yellow-bellied marmots. Males sometimes have large harems, and the females defend the areas around their natal burrows. Even down to occasionally killing each other's young, Columbians live the lives of miniature yellow-bellies, which is sort of what they are. Somewhere far back in time, probably on the Asian Steppes, they branched off of the same family tree.

The story of the golden-mantled ground squirrels is slightly different. They tend not to form large colonies, although they are sometimes polygamous, with more than one female having a burrow within a male's territory. Where Columbians tend to be grazers, heading out into areas of fresh greenery and parking there to eat, golden-mantleds tend to be high-speed gleaners, constantly on the move, zipping around,

GOLDEN-MANTLED GROUND SQUIRREL, BEARTOOTH PLATEAU

picking up choice seeds and tidbits of fresh growth here and there, and then returning to the shelter of their burrow or rocks to eat.

This conglomerate of rocks, tundra, pika, marmots, and ground squirrels is a community. As in any community, there are conflicts: pika hay piles occasionally get raided by marmots or ground squirrels; a marmot bullies a ground squirrel out of a prime feeding area; a golden-mantled ground squirrel or pika dives for cover into a marmot burrow. But close, competitive interactions between the different species are relatively rare, for each of these animals uses the environment a little differently. Each feeds on slightly different types of vegetation, often at different times of day. Each also has different seasonal preferences for a variety of vegetation. For example, late in the summer, pika begin making their hay piles. At this time, ground squirrels' diets are tending toward flower blossoms and seeds, and marmots are after the season's last remaining succulent leaves. The pika, however, needs stuff that will dry out quickly and thoroughly before being stored. Vegetation with too high a moisture content would quickly be attacked by damaging molds and fungi, greatly reducing its nutritional value later on in the winter. So pika go after grasses and sedges, which dry quickly and store well and are exactly the food sources that other talus dwellers are avoiding.

LEFT: ALBINO COLUMBIAN GROUND SQUIRREL, KANANASKIS COUNTRY, SOUTHERN ALBERTA, CANADA
OPPOSITE: GOLDEN-MANTLED GROUND SQUIRREL, BEARTOOTH PLATEAU

Life, death, and time made these determinations. Competition with other species (*interspecific*) was combined with competition within each species (*intraspecific*). Combined with the heavy toll the Pleistocene environment took on each animal, this meant that individuals engaged in fruitless competitive activities with other species found themselves grossly overloaded with conflict and stress, things that seriously cut into the business of foraging and reproduction. These individuals simply died, or failed to reproduce. Then and now, it really all comes down to calories; warmth, reproduction, and hibernation are energy-dependent and energy-intensive. Waste too much on avoidable conflicts and genes do not make it into the future.

There is cooperation within the talus community that goes beyond simple avoidance of conflict. Animals quickly become familiar with one another's alarm calls and patterns of movement. The sudden shrill whistle of a marmot or the alarm chirp of a ground squirrel will send everyone diving for cover. Even small changes, such as a different pattern of foraging behavior, will put others on edge; a marmot absent from its usual feeding session induces extra caution in his feeding companions. As a result, each talus slope has many sets and many types of eyes, ears, and noses, and they are always vigilant.

LEFT: COLUMBIAN GROUND SQUIRREL, LOGAN PASS, GLACIER NATIONAL PARK
OPPOSITE: HOARY MARMOT, BANFF NATIONAL PARK

THE
FEATHERED
COMMUNITY

THE FEATHERED COMMUNITY

The birds of the high country are a unique lot. From the huge, fierce, golden eagle to the tiny American dipper, they represent extremes in avian evolution: the golden eagle is by far the most aggressive of North America's birds of prey. The white-tailed ptarmigan is the most thermally efficient of all birds. The harlequin duck lives and forages in the most turbulent and violent environments of any North American duck. The American dipper is the only North American songbird that has mastered flight both in the air and beneath the bitter cold waters of mountain streams.

Like most birds, their bones are hollow, rigid, lightweight, and supported by an internal weblike lattice. The flight muscles—paired breast, or *pectorals*—are oversized and extremely powerful. Larger skeletal structures such as the hips and skull are riddled with weight-reducing perforations. For most of the year, their genital tracts are atrophied, so small as to be almost undetectable. They become functional only during the breeding season, and the bird is thus burdened with their weight for a few weeks rather than year-round. Digestive tracts are minimal, yet capable of grinding up everything from hard-shelled seeds to shelled mollusks and small bones. Their lungs, small and elaborately looped, allow each breath of air to be circulated several times. This results in a more efficient exchange of oxygen and carbon dioxide than occurs in mammals, with their two-lobed, saclike lungs. And of course, their feathers, the most efficient of insulating materials, also contribute to the effective, lightweight airfoils that are their wings.

RIGHT: WHITE-TAILED PTARMIGAN IN WINTER PLUMAGE, GLACIER NATIONAL PARK
OPPOSITE: WHITE-TAILED PTARMIGAN, LOGAN PASS

Their high-altitude life, however, has dictated a number of specific physiological and behavioral adaptations.

White-tailed Ptarmigan

The white-tailed ptarmigan is the smallest member of the grouse family (Tetraonidae) and lives at the highest elevations: from the Rockies in northern New Mexico, north and west through the Cascades, and up to central Alaska. At the southern end of their range, they are found only at the most lofty altitudes, usually above ten thousand feet, and at the northern extreme, at lower elevations but still almost always in mountainous terrain. The extent of their range very closely parallels that of pika, both in latitude and altitude. The main difference is that in the warmer southern areas, ptarmigan are usually found only in the mountains' coolest microclimates: north-facing slopes, under shaded overhangs, and in moist depressions.

White-tails are superbly adapted to the cold. In fact, their heat-conserving adaptations easily earn them the "Walking Thermos® Bottle" award. Their sensitivity to heat is extreme; they cannot survive air temperatures even as high as their own body temperature, thirty-nine degrees centigrade, for much more than an hour. Returned to a cool environment, they will still often die—their bodies are simply not designed to allow heat to escape. While most birds dissipate heat through their naked feet, the white-tails' feet are heavily feathered, allowing only minute amounts of heat to escape.

Another heat-conserving feature is the counter-current heat exchange system in their legs. Blood on its way down to the feet dumps some of its heat load into blood heading up into the body cavity. Thus, their feet receive only the minimum heat necessary to

maintain normal functions, and the remainder is diverted upward. Most birds pant to reduce heat build-up and so do white-tails, but they have the lowest evaporative heat-transfer rates of any bird tested. They expel very little heat and moisture either when they breathe or through their skin. Extra-thick layers of feathers and down, especially along the back, make the white-tail a particularly tight and thermally efficient package.

These heat-retaining systems are backed up with an adjustable internal thermostat that allows the body temperature to shift downward almost five degrees centigrade without harmful side effects. All of these adaptations have marooned the white-tail in the coldest environments. Even a short flight to a neighboring mountain range, a distance most birds easily handle, would result in a fatal heat build-up for a white-tail.

Each spring, breeding-age male white-tails set up territories of from one-half to two acres in size, the larger ones occupied by the oldest and most aggressive individuals. The terrain throughout these territories is usually a mixture of talus and ledges interspersed with rolling tundra. Single female ptarmigan peruse the males' territories, landing near a male they find suitable as a mate. Sometimes, either before or after the female lands, the male launches into a courtship flight, which includes periodic high-pitched calls. A courtship dance may be part of the male's repertoire, a kind of head-bobbing, strut-your-stuff shuffle punctuated by clucks, coos, and the

occasional screech. The whole process of choosing a mate is a loose, almost casual affair, defined as much by individual style as it is by "hard-wired" behavior. In fact, the quality of a male's territory seems to be more important to the female than his behavior. In some cases, after strolling around the male's territory for a day or two, the female seems to change her mind about the whole arrangement, and leaves. In other cases, the same pair will stay together year after year, courting before they are on their territory. Then together, once the snow starts to melt, they reestablish their territory from previous years. Polygamy has been observed in white-tails as well; an older, dominant male with a large territory may have as many as three females choose him as a mate.

Usually within two weeks of forming a pair, they mate and the female builds a nest. White-tails' simple nests are virtually invisible—a few twigs or leaves, a little down, and two to five eggs nestled in among some rocks or under a ledge. This approach to nest-building is necessary in the high country, where without much cover, an elaborate structure would stand out as a beacon to predators.

Vulnerability to weather is a trade-off for invisibility. In bad years with frequent late snows or heavy rains, many nests are washed out. Although the eggs can survive near-freezing temperatures and the females tenaciously stay put on their eggs through the fiercest storms, the weather often wins. Nest failures can push one hundred percent in a particularly bad year. In good years, only about fifty to seventy-five percent succeed.

The female incubates the eggs for about three weeks, during which time the male may or may not be around. Why some males stay near the nesting

ABOVE: WHITE-TAILED PTARMIGAN, BANFF NATIONAL PARK
OPPOSITE: MALE PTARMIGAN PATROLLING TERRITORY, GLACIER NATIONAL PARK

females is something of a mystery. They don't help with the incubation, although they will occasionally attempt to confront or distract an intruder approaching the nest. The female rarely leaves the nest more than once a day. When she does, it is a slow, elaborate process. First, while still sitting on the nest, she slowly picks bits and pieces of material from around the nest's edge and piles it up neatly in front of her. Then, very slowly and deliberately, she side-steps off the nest and carefully places the material from her pile over the eggs. She then moves away, seeming to flow between the rocks. Watching this whole procedure is like watching the hour hand on a clock—it is done so slowly and smoothly that no single movement has a beginning or an end—the female is gone and the nest disappears into the rocks.

To achieve this invisibility, white-tailed ptarmigan use the lower limits of predators' perception as a defense—they move *beneath* a predator's capacity to detect motion. All animals have a particular range of motion perception. For example, we cannot see the flight of an arrow to a target, nor can we see a plant actually growing. Somewhere between these two speeds, however, we perceive motion. The ptarmigan takes advantage of this physiological quirk.

All the viable eggs hatch at about the same time, and the female and her young promptly leave the nest, heading for moist areas with plenty of fresh vegetation. Young ptarmigan are able to forage almost immediately upon hatching, learning what to eat by following and watching the female closely—if she pecks at something, they peck at it too. As they become more proficient at feeding on their own, the young wander farther from the female, although rarely out of hearing range. If she spies danger, she lets out a series of warning clucks and the scattered young freeze in place, blending in with the tundra.

Female ptarmigan on nest, Glacier National Park

Shortly after the females and chicks leave the nest, the males begin to wander more widely, and territorial boundaries break down. Soon, the tundra is covered with a variety of individuals, broods, and occasionally flocks of foraging white-tails.

Young ptarmigan grow very quickly. At hatching, they weigh only half an ounce. Six weeks later, they weigh twenty times that and have molted through three sets of plumage. By the time they are eight weeks old, they will have reached full adult size of about a pound and will be molting once again, this time into the white winter plumage that is their hallmark. Ptarmigan are among the masters of camouflage.

There are two kinds of camouflage in the natural world, *pattern* and *disruptive*. With pattern camouflage, an animal looks like the background environment; with disruptive, it displays a jumbled pattern of colors and tones that breaks up its outline. Most predators key in on certain shapes when they hunt, the shapes of prey species. When a prey animal's irregular color pattern breaks up its outline, it simply disappears as far as the predator is concerned. There are few better examples of this than the white-tailed ptarmigan's summer plumage. The mottled tan, gray, black, and white pattern makes a still bird all but invisible among the rocks and tundra plants. Each fall, the birds molt out of their disruptive summer camouflage and into their winter whites, a good example of pattern camouflage. In this case, the pattern is pretty simple: all white, like snow. The elegant plumage, so fine it looks like hair, blends almost perfectly with the snow. The only way to pick out these birds in the winter is to follow their tracks until they end in a large feathered lump, or to spot their black eyes against the all-white environment.

The white-tails' seasonal camouflage is so effective that they rarely have to fly to avoid predators. They just sit still. Even when they are approached head-on, they rarely launch into flight. Instead, they move away with a greatly exaggerated slowness, taking carefully measured steps—like a child trying to sneak past a sleeping parent.

Despite the white-tails' superb heat-retaining qualities, they nonetheless have trouble staying warm in the coldest winter weather. They can only survive a couple of hours of direct exposure when the temperature drops to minus twenty degrees Fahrenheit and the wind is screaming. White-tails escape the worst conditions by hunkering down beneath an insulating layer of snow. As storms blow in, they scratch out a small depression in the lee of a rock ledge or Krummholz and let the snow drift in around them until they are completely covered. In some places, where the dense low-lying vegetation forms a support structure for the snow, they burrow down and actually forage beneath the crust. Only when the bitter cold settles in for weeks and the snows are particularly deep or heavily crusted will the ptarmigan move down out of alpine areas and into the trees.

Over a typical winter, sixty to eighty percent of the previous year's young will die. Even among the experienced adults, twenty to forty percent will not survive. These seem like high numbers, and they are, but they're not unusual for the grouse family, or many other families of northern birds for that matter. Birds are borderline warm-blooded creatures. That is, the trait of warm-bloodedness is in its infancy in most avian species. Mammals have developed a sort of metabolic back-up system that stores highly refined carbohydrates and fats in muscles, bones, and organs throughout the body. These reserves are constantly available to provide on-demand energy for movement and temperature regulation. Most birds, however, carry minimal reserves, stored in the muscles used for movement, particularly flight. Without good reserves, they rely heavily on the energy derived from food being digested in their stomachs. Empty stomach, no energy. No energy, no warmth. For the white-tailed

ptarmigan, and many other northern birds, going to bed without their dinner can be fatal.

Throughout their range, white-tails have been hunted for both sport and food. This is unfortunate, for with their high natural overwinter mortality rates, additional mortality from hunting is enough to wipe out a population. Apparently this is exactly what happened in the mid- to late nineteenth century throughout the southern half of the Rockies. Early explorers and settlers in the region reported enormous flocks, numbering well into the hundreds (one flock on Colorado's Mount Evans was estimated at over five hundred). Unfortunately, white-tails are tasty and easy to kill. Their camouflage and sit-tight tactics served them poorly against humans, and by the early twentieth century, many populations were decimated or eliminated. Today, although one can no longer see flocks of hundreds, several western states (most notably Colorado) have engaged in aggressive transplanting efforts, successfully reestablishing the ptarmigan throughout much of its traditional range.

Harlequin Duck

Every region has its living jewels, bright flashes of colorful life that flit by in the underbrush, through the branches, or beneath the waves. The jewels of the high country, bobbing and diving through the most treacherous mountain torrents, are the harlequin ducks. Early each spring, these spectacular little birds leave their wintering grounds along the violent, rocky coast of the northern Pacific and fly hundreds of miles inland to equally violent and rocky mountain streams to breed. They are the first splash of

color to grace the high country, confirmation that spring is about to arrive.

With casual indifference, the elegant drakes and drab hens negotiate bone-cracking rapids, fearlessly diving into standing waves to feed along the bottom, just as they fed in pounding surf along ocean shores. No North American bird is more closely tied to white water than the harlequin duck. But why white water? Why risk pulverization on a daily basis? The answer is food, lots of it. Tremendous amounts of air are pumped and pounded into the water and fresh supplies of nutrients are constantly circulated. Given someplace to escape direct assault by waves and currents (or the ability to build their own bomb shelter, as do mussels and limpets), small organisms flourish in these oxygen-rich environments. Down among the nooks and crannies of rocky ocean shores and along the bottoms of mountain streams live entire elaborate invertebrate communities, complete with plants, grazers, filter-feeders, and predators, scuttling around just out of the ripping current's reach. Enter the harlequin, the most efficient, durable, and powerful North American diving duck and the only one able to forage in this environment, and you have what amounts to a private duck smorgasbord. Using their oversized feet and pumping with their wings, harlequins power their way down to the bottom and root around among the rocks with their stout bills.

The harlequins found in the high country of the West winter in the Pacific from the Aleutians, south down the coast of Alaska and British Columbia, to northern California. There are also separate Pacific populations along the Siberian coast and small Atlantic populations edging the coasts of southeastern Canada, the northeastern U.S., Iceland, and Greenland.

Throughout their range, harlequins breed only on clear mountain or tundra streams. In the high mountains of North America, they select streams in the Rockies from Wyoming north, and from northern

Oregon up through the Cascades, the coastal ranges of Washington and British Columbia, and much of Alaska. The drakes court the hens year-round, and pairs are usually established while the birds are still on the ocean. They arrive on their breeding streams between late April and early May, and the males court the females for another two to three weeks before they mate. During this time of courtship, the drake will defend the hen from intruding bachelor males.

Little is known about the social position of these bachelors. They could be young males who have just reached maturity, are returning to their natal streams, and are going through the motions of breeding and courting, a sort of dry run. Or they may be older males who have lost their mates but their instinct drives them back to their former breeding streams. Perhaps they're opportunists, the duck version of a lounge lizard, hoping to entice a female who has lost or is separated from her mate.

Regardless, males with mates spend a fair amount of time keeping these bachelors away from them. Usually, some serious head bobbing is enough to let the intruder know he's not wanted, but if this display fails to drive him off, the protective male will attack head-on, nipping with his beak and thumping with his wings. These conflicts usually end quickly, with the intruder beating a squeaking retreat before any damage is done.

Harlequins are not territorial; rather, pairs typically work their way up and down a half- to one-mile stretch of stream that they do not defend against other ducks. Pairs with overlapping ranges frequently pass on the stream and seem to go out of their way to ignore each other.

LEFT: HARLEQUIN HEN, GLACIER NATIONAL PARK
OPPOSITE: HARLEQUIN DRAKE, GLACIER NATIONAL PARK

After a pair mates in late May or early June, sometimes bobbing down through rapids during the act, the female lays her eggs within about a week. The nest is usually a down-lined cup nestled among rocks along the stream shore or on an island. (This isn't always the case, though—sometimes they nest in tree cavities or on cliff ledges.) Nesting success is very closely tied to the severity and timing of spring runoff. In years when runoff is high and peaks during nesting season, virtually all of the nests on a stream can be wiped out. In milder years, up to eighty percent of nests succeed.

The hens incubate the eggs for roughly three weeks. It is during this time that the males abandon the mountains and head back to the ocean. Because the females leave their nests only to feed, the mountain streams can suddenly seem virtually empty of harlequins.

Brood sizes typically range from two to five young. Immediately on hatching, the ducklings are ushered out onto the stream by the female. For the first month of their lives, the ducklings stay in slow water as the hen gradually works them up to the torrents and waves that will dominate the rest of their lives. The young are competent white-water river-runners by the time they are six weeks old, and fledge at around eight weeks. Migration back to the ocean begins in mid-August, and by the end of the month, the mountain streams are once again empty of harlequins.

The harlequins of North America are not doing well. Canada declared them endangered along its Atlantic coast in 1990, and in 1991, they became candidates for the Endangered Species List in the U.S. Throughout their North American range, these tough little ducks are facing man-caused threats both on the oceans and at their breeding streams. Harlequin wintering grounds along ocean coasts are exactly where pollutants, such as oil from spills, collect. These pollutants are both absorbed directly by the ducks and concentrated in their preferred foods, crustaceans and mussels. Throw in the occasional disaster, and an already-challenging life can become impossible. Following the Exxon *Valdez* spill, virtually all harlequins tested in Prince William Sound from 1989 to 1993 had high concentrations of petrochemicals in their tissues. One study found virtually no signs of successful harlequin reproduction in oily western areas for the four years following the spill.

Harlequin breeding streams are under constant attack from a variety of other sources as well. The practice of clearcut logging can make a river, or even an entire drainage, uninhabitable for the ducks when excessive siltation smothers their food supply. Increased runoff and sediment load in streams below clearcuts can literally choke an aquatic community to death, making the harlequins' specialized feeding abilities all but worthless—there simply is nothing for them to eat under the waves.

Another threat comes from overcrowding on breeding streams. Not too many ducks, but too many people, outdoorsy, nature-loving, people who are turning in ever-increasing numbers to white water for their thrills. The best time of year for rafting and kayaking is in the spring, when the water is high and fast. This often puts humans in the same place at the same time as harlequins attempting to breed. Several studies have shown a direct correlation between high levels of human activity and low harlequin breeding-success rates on streams in Grand Teton National Park and on popular recreational rivers such as the St. Joe in Idaho and the Maligne in Jasper National Park, Canada.

HARLEQUIN HEN WITH FAMILY, GLACIER NATIONAL PARK

The solution seems pretty simple; we have the option of putting off our activities until a later date but the harlequins don't. If we want to continue to be dazzled by their colors on rushing mountain streams, we need to give them the room they need to increase their numbers.

American Dipper

Dippers are something of an anomaly. They are *passerines*, perching birds, just like robins, wrens, sparrows, and other commonly seen varieties. They have, however, opted for a very ducklike lifestyle, often sharing the harlequin's waterways. Dippers live their entire lives in the water or on its edge; even when they fly, they are rarely more than a couple of feet above the water's surface. They stay on their streams

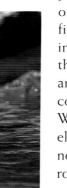

year-round, migrating in the winter only far enough down-drainage to find open water. Unlike most passerines, they sing even in the winter; their melodious, rambling twitter is an extraordinary contrast to the bitter cold and gray of the lean season. Where harlequins are glittering jewels, dippers are the very definition of nondescript. The slate gray of wet rocks, they blend in extremely well on the rare occasions when they stop doing knee bends and remain still. Dippers dip. Since they are drab and blend in well with the wet rocks along their streams, dipping allows them to make themselves visible to others on demand. Sit still and they remain hidden from a predator. Start dipping and singing and they can declare ownership of a territory or court a mate.

Dippers are exceptional divers. Without the benefit of webbed feet, using only their wings to propel them-

selves downward, these apple-sized birds can dive to depths of over twelve feet and remain on the bottom for thirty seconds or more. Using aquadynamics, they orient their bodies and wings so that the current presses them to the bottom, where they use their legs and pump their wings to push themselves along among the rocks. While there, they root around for invertebrates such as stonefly, caddis, and dragonfly larvae, much as harlequins do. The two species compete for some of the same foods, but in general, the dipper forages in much slower and usually shallower waters than are frequented by harlequins.

So how does a little songbird survive icy mountain waters? Like virtually all birds, the dipper has a gland, the *uropygial*, at the base of its tail that secretes oil. During preening, birds reach back and pinch the gland and then smear the oil on the sides of their beaks. They then apply this oil to their feathers, opening their beaks and gently drawing individual quills through. Dippers generate more than eight times the oil of a typical passerine and can cover themselves liberally, creating virtually waterproof plumage. The outer feather layer is relatively coarse, much like that of other birds, but there is also an underlayer of particularly fine, dense down next to the body, which provides tremendous insulation. Like other birds, dippers also have a semi-transparent inner eyelid, the *nictitating membrane*, which closes over their eyes and may function like built-in swimming goggles when they dive. Unlike many other diving birds that have developed permanently sealed nostrils, dippers have flaps, *opercula*, that they can close to prevent water from entering their lungs.

Left and opposite: American dippers, Glacier National Park

Dippers of both sexes are territorial, staking out stretches of stream usually about a quarter- to half-mile long. During the breeding season, early spring to mid-summer, a female moves into an adjoining male's territory and announces her presence by dipping. The male flies to her and once on the ground in front of her, aims his head straight up while he prances about and sings. During the courtship period, roughly a week, the female builds a moss nest with one small opening right at the water's edge, under an overhang or behind a waterfall. After the pair mates, she lays three to five eggs and does all of the incubating alone. Within about two weeks, the eggs hatch and both adults share in feeding the young. After another two to three weeks, the young leave the nest and are diving, flying, and feeding on their own, although they stay in the male's territory soliciting food for as long as he tolerates them.

Dippers practice what is called serial polygamy—both adults now repeat the courtship process with new partners. They nest again, the female moving on to a new male's territory. There are not many figures on dipper population dynamics, but birds with such high reproductive rates usually have very high juvenile mortality rates, often well above seventy-five percent. Some of this mortality almost surely comes from a lack of foraging experience, which leads to starvation or accidents underwater. There is also a fair amount of anecdotal evidence indicating that dippers face significant predation by large fish. A fly fisherman on the Yellowstone River in Montana recalled watching a dipper flit from rock to rock. According to the fisherman, the bird perched right in front of him and began preening. Fascinated, the man stopped fishing and bent forward to watch. Suddenly, the water just downstream of the rock exploded, and in one smooth motion, an enormous cutthroat trout arched out of the water, engulfed the dipper, and sailed over the rock to the upstream side.

The event took place so close to the fisherman that water splashed his face. Regardless of the story's accuracy, large rainbow, brook, bull, and cutthroat trout as well as pike are easily capable of taking dippers as prey.

Golden Eagle

The golden eagle is the most formidable predator in North America's skies. Even our nation's symbol, the bald eagle, quickly defers to a golden arriving at a carcass. With up to a seven-and-one-half-foot wingspan, three-inch talons backed by a grip powerful enough to break a man's forearm, and an eighty-mile-per-hour attack speed, they are by far the high country's deadliest predators. A typical golden eagle weighs from eight to twelve pounds and can carry nearly half that amount. Ground squirrels and marmots, mountain sheep lambs, mountain goat kids, and caribou fawns are on the golden eagle's menu. In some cases, yearlings and weak adults are killed by hungry eagles, either by being suddenly yanked off cliffs or repeatedly punctured around the head and neck with those deadly talons.

Goldens are circumpolar, found throughout the northern hemisphere wherever there are large expanses of wild lands. In North America, they are found primarily in broken country, badlands, chaparral, and mountains from Mexico north throughout the western U.S. and Canada to Alaska and the Arctic. They are mainly open-country and mountain hunters, relying on their phenomenal eyesight to spot distant prey long before they themselves are seen. One

GOLDEN EAGLE, SOUTHERN BRITISH COLUMBIA. THE EYES OF THE GOLDEN EAGLE HAVE ROUGHLY EIGHT TIMES THE RESOLUTION OF THE HUMAN EYE, AS WELL AS THE ABILITY TO CHANGE POWER, MUCH LIKE A ZOOM LENS ON A CAMERA.

researcher in Idaho's Birds of Prey National Wildlife Refuge saw a golden eagle on a high cliff suddenly turn and stare at something in the distance. The eagle then launched into a straight glide, stooped, and struck an animal on the plateau. Using a range finder, the researcher judged the distance from cliff to victim at over a mile. The eagle then returned to the cliff with its prey, which turned out to be a ground squirrel. From more than a mile away, the movement of a ten-inch-tall rodent had caught the bird's attention.

Raptors, birds of prey, have amazing visual acuity. The rods and cones on their retinas, the cells that receive light, are so densely packed that they have roughly eight times the resolution of the human eye. What this means is that if birds could read a standard eye chart, they would have 20/2.5 vision: they can see at twenty feet what an average human has to be at two and one-half feet to see. In addition, there is a bony structure, called the *sclerotic ring*, circling the front of the eyeball. The bird can force its eyeball forward, into, and through this ring, effectively elongating the eye and increasing the focal length, much like a zoom lens. Behind these remarkable eyes, oversized optic nerves pipe information directly into the *wulst*, the largest portion of the bird's brain and also the section devoted to processing complex visual signals.

Recent research reveals that at least some raptors can see ultraviolet light. These high-flying birds scan a landscape on which they cannot only see tiny prey, but can also see where prey has recently been. Fresh urine absorbs enough ultraviolet light to be visible as dark patches to the raptors, and concentrations of urine reveal an abundance of otherwise-hidden prey.

Goldens nest in the spring, April in the far north and as early as January or February in the south. The same pair usually returns to the same area or nest site

Golden eagle, Southern British Columbia

each year and may mate for life. Unlike some species of geese, which pine away until they die if they lose a mate, goldens are pragmatic, immediately searching for a replacement if their mate is lost or killed. In harsh early experiments, researchers killed females on their nests and took the eggs, and new mates were on the scene and was accepted or being courted by the males in a matter of days. Overall, golden populations in North America appear to be stable. In many environments, the number of goldens is limited by the number of suitable nesting territories; somewhere out on the fringes, individuals soar, looking for available mates and nest sites, waiting for a chance to reproduce.

Once a pair arrives in their territory, they build a nest or add to an existing one, usually on a south-facing cliff to catch the first sun of the morning. The nest can be up to five feet across and is usually made of a tangle of sticks and heavy brush. During the nest-building phase, the male courts the female, passing pieces of food and nesting material to her in the air. When the nest nears completion, the pair mates on the wing. Locked together, they tumble earthward from hundreds of feet up, often completing the act and separating just as they are about to strike the ground.

The fertilized eggs descend single-file from the female's ovary down the oviduct. Like most birds, only her left ovary is fully functional; the right, which is much smaller and does not produce eggs, probably serves only as a hormone-producing gland. As the egg descends, the shell forms around it in layers. First, the shell's inner membrane is formed in the oviduct, and then lower, in the uterus, the hard outer shell is laid down. As each egg is completed, it is deposited in the nest. The whole process, from mating to finished egg, takes only a couple of days, and the female is burdened with the weight of a whole egg for just a few hours. The typical clutch size is two, but can be as few as one to as many as four. The female incubates the eggs with little or no help from the male for about thirty-five days; there is some evidence that in colder northern climates, the eggs take seven to ten days longer to mature. During this time, the male hunts virtually all day long, providing food for his mate.

The eggs hatch asynchronously, usually in the order they were laid, separated by one to three days. This staggered hatching serves much the same purpose as delayed implantation in mammals, allowing the quantity of available food and other environmental conditions to determine the number of young. (For a discussion of delayed implantation in mammals,

MYTH AND SYMBOLISM SURROUND THE GOLDEN EAGLE. IN NATIVE AMERICAN LORE, IT IS EQUIVALENT OF THE PHOENIX, THE SYMBOL OF REBIRTH—NOT JUST REBIRTH IN THE SENSE OF AN AFTERLIFE, BUT THE REBIRTH ONE EXPERIENCES AFTER DEFEAT, WHETHER SPIRITUAL OR PHYSICAL. THE PHOENIX IS OFTEN DEPICTED RISING FROM FLAMES AND ASHES, FREE, PROUD AND STRONGER THAN BEFORE. IN MEDIEVAL EUROPE, THE GOLDEN'S LIKENESS GRACED SHIELDS AND BANNERS. IT WAS THE WAR BIRD, A SYMBOL OF FEROCITY AND POWER. FROM ANCIENT REVERENCE, WE GO TO MODERN NORTH AMERICAN STORIES ABOUT GOLDENS CARRYING OFF WHOLE SHEEP, OR EVEN SMALL CHILDREN. AS RECENTLY AS THE 1950S, ENTIRE REGIONS OF THE COUNTRY WERE THROWN INTO PANIC AS RUMORS OF GOLDEN EAGLES SNATCHING CHILDREN FROM BACKYARDS CIRCULATED AND WERE PUBLISHED IN THE PRESS. ANY HAWK OR EAGLE SOARING OVER A SOUTHWESTERN SUBURB WAS ENOUGH TO STOP ALL OUTDOOR PLAY FOR THE REST OF THE DAY.

see page 95.) The aggression of the first hatchling is primarily determined by how well it is fed. If food is in short supply, it is extremely aggressive and may kill other nestlings. If food is plentiful, it leaves its younger and smaller siblings alone. After the eggs hatch, both adults become nearly full-time hunters, scrambling to provide for ravenous and rapidly growing chicks.

The chicks develop from a few ounces at hatching to over six pounds in only two months, a twenty-four-fold increase in weight. At nine to ten weeks, the young fledge, taking their first short flights. At three months, they are hunting and taking game on their own. The family will stay together until late in the fall, and then the young wander off on their own, sometimes traveling over a thousand miles from where they were hatched. The first year is very tough for young goldens. Mortality—from causes varying from starvation and disease to shooting, poisoning, and electrocution on power lines—is anywhere from fifty to eighty percent. Even automobiles pose a serious threat; inexperienced birds often stuff themselves on roadkill and are hit by cars as they struggle to take off. If they can survive their first, trying years, goldens may live as long as forty years, although the average is probably somewhere in the mid-teens to twenties.

There is increasing evidence that raptors are capable of much more sophisticated reasoning than they have been given credit for in the past. Different populations and even different individuals develop hunting tactics that rival those of social mammals. Two particular cooperative hunting methods are frequently used by goldens when pursuing high-country prey. When a pair of birds is hunting, one will soar fairly high and in plain sight of the ground, perhaps over a mountain cirque. This bird is almost always spotted immediately by all of the marmots, ground squirrels, and nanny goats with young kids, and alarm calls and whistles are exchanged. As long as the bird keeps its distance, nobody dives for cover. They watch the bird closely—too closely. Somewhere, zooming along low and fast, following the contours of the mountain, is the decoy's mate. Before it knows what hit it, one of the cirque's inhabitants will have been struck by the second eagle and the high eagle will be diving down to share in the feast.

The other method is a little more direct. Two goldens cruise along together at low altitude, spooking prey animals as they go. Sooner or later, the birds surprise something at close range and the victim dives for whatever cover is at hand. If the cover doesn't provide much protection, one eagle lands and walks in after the victim in an attempt to flush it out into the open, while the second either perches or soars nearby. If the prey is young or inexperienced, it will often bolt from cover, right into the second eagle's talons—another successful hunt.

GOLDEN EAGLE, SOUTHERN BRITISH COLUMBIA

BIGHORN RAM AND EWE, GLACIER NATIONAL PARK

THE HOOFED COMMUNITY

THE HOOFED COMMUNITY

Four species of large grazers make their homes in the high country: the mountain goat; mountain caribou; bighorn sheep; and the thinhorn, or Dall's, sheep. All are referred to as ungulates, a broad term for hoofed animals. They are ruminants, meaning that, similar to domestic cattle, they have two or more stomachs. Each stomach is a small ecosystem containing varieties of bacteria capable of digesting cellulose, the material that makes up the cell wall of most plants. With the help of these bacteria, ruminants can survive on vegetation that provides very little nutritional value because—similar to the fermentation process we use to make beer and wine—the bacteria turn cellulose into sugars. These bacteria not only help with the digestion of plants but themselves are food for the ruminant.

As bacteria populations grow, they overflow and are carried downstream in the digestive tract, where they in turn are digested, adding protein to the animal's system. If the ruminant can't find enough to eat, not only it but also the bacteria starve. At that point, no matter how much food it finds, it often will die anyway; once the bacteria are gone, the ruminant has no way to digest its food and can literally starve to death on a full stomach. Unfortunately for many high-country grazers, semi-starvation is an annual event.

In the fall, ruminants are at their peak physical condition, having spent the summer grazing on nutrient-rich, succulent greens. When the first frosts hit, most plants stop pumping nutrients up out of their roots and the above-ground portion of the plant either dies or goes dormant, leaving little of

Bighorn rams in blizzard, Glacier National Park

any nutritional value for the grazer to eat. By the time the snows pile up, most ruminants are beginning to lose weight, despite grazing and browsing eighteen hours a day or more. In late winter, browse, grasses, and sedges have lost up to seventy-five percent of their crude protein and almost all calcium and phosphate—little or no nutritional value is left for the grazer. The ungulate's body then turns on itself, using fat deposits and robbing bones of critical minerals, causing them to become more porous and brittle and greatly increasing the chance of a serious break. Winter then becomes a desperate metabolic sprint to springtime, a race against disappearing physical reserves, thinning forage of decreasing nutritional value, declining internal bacteria populations, and a slowly dissolving skeleton.

The ungulates of the mountains, these products of Pleistocene glacial ages, are descendants of the toughest of their kind and have a surprising ally in their battle for survival: the wind. Enormous weather systems slam into the spines of the mountains, literally piling up and then bursting through passes and pouring over ridges, roaring down valleys and slopes with tremendous speed. These howling hurricane-force winds relentlessly tear heat away from warm bodies but also sweep the slopes clear of snow, exposing vegetation.

High-country grazers often seek out the most blustery, windswept slopes for their winter ranges, shunning deep snows in the valleys and drifted-in leeward mountain faces. Typical winter range for many of these ungulates is a south-facing, sun-catching slope with broken terrain, ranging from thirty degrees to vertical and running parallel to the predominant winds. The wind, incline, and angle to the sun means that these slopes are the last to be covered with snow each fall and the first to green-up each spring.

The influence of these winds cannot be too heavily stressed. When we hear wind-chill factors on the weather report, the numbers are usually somewhere in the minus-ten to minus-forty-degrees Fahrenheit range. If the same reports were given for areas frequented by high-country wildlife, the numbers would range from minus seventy-five to minus one hundred-eighty degrees Fahrenheit. While wind is an ally, it is not a friend—these low temperatures are deadly and any animal not well insulated and without shelter will perish. Fortunately, these slopes are usually covered with breaks, nooks, and ledges that offer some protection from the winds; animals congregate in these places, hunkering down to wait out the worst blows.

Despite their remarkably stout constitutions, many high-country ungulates die each winter. The same wind that exposes food also robs the animals of heat and calories. Minor infections can explode into deadly diseases in a winter-weakened body. The already treacherous, precipitous terrain is coated with snow and ice. Moving from feeding area to feeding area involves crossing unstable slopes and avalanche chutes, and these brutal conditions dominate the high country for seven to nine months of the year.

Typical overwinter mortality rates range from twenty to one hundred percent for juveniles and ten to forty percent for adults. Each spring thaw reveals the crumpled bodies of avalanche and fall victims and the emaciated carcasses of those who succumbed to disease or starvation. Their bodies provide a valuable source of calories for predators and scavengers such as grizzly, coyote, wolverine, and golden eagles, often tipping the scales in favor of life over starvation for the carnivore.

In the face of all of this hardship, it's strange to see the young of these creatures engaged in what seems to be reckless, calorie-wasting play each spring. Why waste energy on play when it could be put into growth or into fat reserves that will see the animal through the vicious winter ahead? The answer is that

growth and fat reserves are only part of the survival equation. The high country also demands grace, agility, power, and stamina in its inhabitants, and those deficient in these areas will probably not survive their first winter.

Mountain goat kids and mountain sheep lambs go out of their way to climb on and bound over chunks of rock or even a sleeping parent. Mountain caribou young course across open tundra on long, ungainly legs and oversized feet, developing the stamina that is the hallmark of their kind. Other forms of play mimic adult social interactions, such as the head-to-head combat of mountain sheep rams and caribou bulls or goats' twirling head-to-rump battles. While they are young, with only little nubs of antlers or horns, these mock battles are harmless, but have serious implications: they are the beginnings of the ritualized behaviors that will dominate interactions with their own kind for the rest of their lives.

Why do social or ritualized behaviors exist? Why not pull out all the stops and eliminate your rivals so that you never again have to waste time and energy dealing with them? While it is true that death is the occasional result of battles between ungulates, it is not the norm. The reasons are fairly simple: equipment and the risk of retaliation. These animals have headgear that is as much ornamental as it is functional. Unlike the down-to-business hardware of carnivores, most ungulates' antlers and horns are poorly suited for killing. Further, if they were put to such deadly use, the aggressor could find himself on the receiving end of a retaliatory attack. Add to this the tremendous demands of the high-altitude environment, particularly the winter, and extreme aggression with its associated tolls is a distinct disadvantage.

BIGHORN RAM, JASPER NATIONAL PARK, ALBERTA, CANADA

Mountain Sheep

Two species of mountain sheep clamber the crags of North America's high country. The all-white Dall's sheep makes its home in the far north, from arctic Alaska's Brooks Range south to the Kenai Peninsula and east roughly to the Yukon–Northwest Territory border. A dark-bodied subspecies, called Stone's sheep, roams from south-central Yukon down into the Cassiars and northern Rockies of British Columbia. Collectively, Dall's and Stone's are referred to as the thinhorn sheep, as their horns are less massive, although often longer, than the heavy horns of the mountain bighorn. The second species of high country mountain sheep, the mountain bighorn, range from just north of Jasper National Park, south through the Rockies and outlying ranges to southern New Mexico, and in the badlands of South Dakota.

The lineage and classification of North American mountain sheep has been the subject of controversy. At one time, U.S. biologists classified them all as bighorns, considering both Dall's and Stone's sheep to have derived directly from bighorn stock. The Canadians classified bighorns and Dall's as separate species, with Stone's a subspecies of Dall's (the most widely accepted modern classification). Russian biologists had their own ideas; some believed that Siberian snow sheep, Dall's, and Stone's were related but that bighorn developed from a completely different stock. They reached these conclusions based in part on the reasonable assumption that migration across Beringia was cross-directional and that recent ancestors of both the modern Dall's and Siberian snow sheep intermingled as recently as the last glacial age. They could be right, although recent genetic testing has revealed enough fundamental differences between the chromosomes of Siberian snow sheep and Dall's

to warrant each having their own species designation. This does not eliminate the possibility of a common ancestor, however.

The Pelly Mountains in southern Yukon Territory are a fairly clear geographic dividing line between Dall's and Stone's sheep ranges. Only Dall's can be found north and west of the Pellys, whereas Stone's sheep range from the Pellys south. Northern Stone's sheep have light-colored wool, while at the southern end, they are nearly black. A silvery Stone's sheep is found in the Pellys; given the common name "Fannin," they are not recognized as genetically different from Stone's. This gradation may be due to the intermingling of Dall's and Stone's sheep in the Pelly region and a subsequent southward flow of Dall's genes. Interestingly, the opposite, a northward movement of Stone's sheep and a trend towards darker Dall's sheep at the southern end of their range, does not seem to be happening.

Bighorn ancestors probably crossed Beringia three or more glacial ages ago and migrated southward in front of advancing ice. During a subsequent interglacial period, they made the jump eastward to the Rocky Mountains and the Great Plains, spreading both north and south along the interior mountains and plains. During subsequent bouts of glaciation, these mountain sheep were repeatedly cut off from their plains- and desert-dwelling kin, which put them on a different evolutionary track, one specific to their environment. The results are visible today upon comparison of desert bighorn with their mountain cousins. Desert bighorn have a lean and rangy look, leggy and relatively slight. In contrast, mountain sheep are heavier and stockier—the cold temperature of the mountains places a premium on large body size.

Rams are massive and powerful beasts. While the largest bighorns can weigh 300 pounds, they typically run about 225 to 250 pounds. The thinhorns— Dall's and Stone's—can weigh up to 250 pounds,

averaging around 200. Ewes tend to be about half to two-thirds the size of the rams. Both sexes grow horns, but the females' are more delicate and considerably shorter and smaller in diameter than the rams'. They also stop growing long before they begin to curl.

Rams' horns are a very different story. These stout, curled horns and the skulls from which they grow are superbly designed to deliver and receive enormous impact. Early naturalists believed that the horns' rigid outer layers were made of compressed hair, since they often found hairs wedged into cracks and grooves on the horns' surfaces. Actually, the horns are composed of an outer sheath made of keratins (the same types of protein found in hair and fingernail material) over-laying a short, solid, bony core growing directly out of the skull. Horns grow by adding an annual layer of sheath material directly over the core. Each layer grows under the one before it, resulting in a horn that is essentially a series of nested cones. Where each new cone meets the layer above it, there is a visible growth ring. Until the ram begins to break off horn tips during dominance battles, his age can be estab-lished simply by counting the rings; this method has a plus- or minus-one–year accuracy.

The outer sheath feels like rigid plastic, and under extreme impact or pressure, will flex and bend slightly, absorbing shock. Beneath the horns and across the forehead, the rams' skulls are double layered, the two layers separated by a dense web of shock-absorbing, bony, cross-linked "struts." The skin on the forehead is extremely tough—almost a quarter-inch thick. Taken together, this construction makes for one heavy-duty head.

Mountain sheep horns seem to play a role in the animals' ability to regulate their temperature. Several researchers, while handling stressed or overheated sheep, have noted that the horns get very hot. A

BIGHORN RAM, JASPER NATIONAL PARK

dense web of veins and capillaries overlays the bony core of each horn and carries nutrients to the growing sheath. These blood vessels dilate when the animal overheats, passing heat outward and dissipating it over the horns' large surface area. Some researchers have concluded that an incidental function of the horns may be to act as big, curled, heat sinks. This helps explain how an animal so well adapted to life in the frigid high country can have very close relatives that are able to live in some of North America's hottest desert environments. Desert bighorn ewes have considerably longer horns than mountain bighorn ewes, and desert bighorn rams tend to have longer (though less massive and thinner) horns than mountain bighorn rams. In hot environments natural selection may favor horns that combine a reduction in heat-storing mass with maximum surface area for heat dissipation.

Sheep society is basically divided into two social groups: sexually mature rams and all others. These castes remain separated most of the year by either keeping to themselves in fairly well-defined bands or seasonally migrating to different grazing ranges. The separate groups then migrate to the same area during the fall mating season, or rut. There are few hard-and-fast rules when it comes to seasonal migration. Some sheep remain on essentially the same range year-round, while others have separate winter, summer, fall, and rutting grounds that they cycle through like clockwork (rut areas also tend to be ewe wintering territories). Even within one region's population, individual bands often have different local migration patterns.

Near the end of May, after a 175-day gestation period, pregnant ewes move off by themselves into steep cliffs. In isolation they bear their young, usually one but occasionally twin lambs of about seven pounds. The newborns are precocious, and in a matter of days are bounding around on the rocks and on and over their mothers. Several days after giving birth, the ewes descend to gentler terrain and form large maternity bands. These are usually composed of adolescent (one- and two-year-old) sheep of both sexes, mature ewes without young, and ewes with newborn lambs. Within the band, the current crop of offspring consolidate into romping, roving play groups. Joined by the occasional juvenile, they engage in mock dominance battles and leaping chases among boulders and talus. These groups wander surprising distances from the ewes, and it is fairly common to see groups with no adults anywhere in sight (although bands this far out do display a visible collective anxiety).

Within the groups composed of ewes and juveniles, there is a fair amount of ritualized behavior, particularly among young males, but a strict hierarchy is not maintained. Any ewe purposefully leading her lamb off to a feeding area can become leader-for-a-day if enough others decide to follow her. Rams, however, maintain a clearly defined dominance hierarchy among themselves year-round through elaborate, highly ritualized behavior. Each group is led by one especially large-horned, large-bodied individual. Even if several rams of almost equal size and status are in the same band, there will be only one clear leader and surprisingly, he is on the receiving end of most of the overtly aggressive interactions. These dominant rams almost never use their horns as weapons except during the rut; they prove their status by easily accepting and absorbing the head-on blows of lesser rams. Lower-ranking rams use any advantage they can to increase their impact, sometimes even launching themselves from ledges above their opponent. Regardless of the force of the blow, there seems to be little residual effect from this aggression—after the two clash, the lesser ram will often nuzzle the dominant ram. By the same token, the dominant does not retaliate with clashes of his own.

In both ewe and ram groups, there are eight easily recognized and oft-repeated behaviors associated with the majority of social interactions: the lo stretch;

present, or present threat; lip curl; neck fight; horning; front kick; ramming or butting; and mounting. It should be noted that a behavior may mean different things in different situations. This is particularly true for maintenance behaviors, which are not message-sending symbolic moves or sounds, but rather routine daily-life activities: grooming, eating, mating, and drinking.

Symbolic social behaviors, those designed to convey a message from one individual to another, often borrow movements from maintenance behaviors. For example, in some species of ducks, a lone male dipping his bill into the water and then throwing his head back simply means he's drinking. The same motion in the presence of a female means he's courting her and is interested in sex. In the presence of a rival male, the motion signifies aggression and amounts to a "back off" signal.

A similar situation occurs among mountain sheep rams and has led to a fair amount of controversy. There are researchers who feel that the mounting behavior of dominant rams indicates that rams are homosexual outside of the rut. There is, however, virtually no evidence that mounting behavior within ram bands is for the purpose of sexual gratification. Rather, mounting is virtually always performed in association with dominance displays, and rarely by a subordinate to a dominant. If mounting were for the purpose of sex, we would expect subordinate rams to regularly attempt to mount dominant rams, just as these subordinates regularly attempt to mount ewes during the rut, but they don't. While true homosexuality and bisexuality do occur in virtually all higher animals, and possibly in mountain sheep, they do not play a significant role in the structure of typical ram bands.

Both ewes and rams perform the *lo stretch* and it is

most often directed by a dominant toward a subordinate. The dominant animal extends its head out and down, often cocked at a slight angle, as it approaches or passes the lower-ranking individual. Often, that's all there is to it—it seems to be a sort of swagger, a way of reaffirming who's boss. On other occasions it's a "get out of my way" signal used by the dominant to move a lower-ranking animal out of a preferred bedding site or to usurp desirable forage. During the rut, rams perform the lo stretch as a courtship signal as they approach estrous ewes and also as a challenge to rival or subordinate males.

The *present* is almost exclusively performed by rams. The ram cocks and slightly twists his back, showing off his horns to a rival or subordinate ram or perhaps to a ewe he is courting. At other times, a dominant ram will stand in the middle of a group of lower-ranked individuals and present, which initiates another behavior, called *horning*, or rubbing. Horning is virtually always performed by subordinates on dominants. The subordinate rubs its face and horns against the face and horns of the dominant. This seems to have a double purpose: first, it's sort of like kissing the king's ring, an acknowledgment of lower status. Second, the dominant ram secretes a scent from the preorbital glands (immediately below each eye), and the rams who rub his face will be impregnated with his scent, the olfactory equivalent to gang colors or a tattoo. There is evidence that sheep are active throughout the night, and this scent may make locating the rest of the band a little easier, reducing the need for constant reintroduction and status testing. This could be particularly valuable for mountain sheep in the far north, who spend a great deal of time foraging in winter's almost perpetual darkness.

Neck fights are usually associated with other dominance displays, such as the lo stretch and present, and are almost always performed by rams. The animal attempting to assert dominance will rest its head across the back of the subordinate. When two individuals are nearly equal in status, they will jockey for position, interspersing a present with attempts to lay their heads across their opponents' backs. Occasionally, other sheep will join in, and two or three sheep, even subordinates, will wind up resting their heads on one sheep's back. This behavior also seems to be used by subordinates to get a quick "dominance fix." While two dominant sheep engage in a neck fight, a subordinate will sometimes slide in and slyly rest his head across the back of one of his superiors.

OPPOSITE, LEFT: BIGHORN RAMS IN GLACIER NATIONAL PARK. THE RAM OF THE LEFT IS PERFORMING THE LO STRETCH. OPPOSITE, RIGHT: THE RAM ON THE LEFT IS PERFORMING A LO STRETCH WITH PRESENT, AND THE RAM ON THE RIGHT IS DOING A CLASSIC PRESENT. JASPER NATIONAL PARK RIGHT: BIGHORN RAMS HORNING, GLACIER NATIONAL PARK

The *lipcurl* is probably not a behavioral display, even though it is most often associated with other intense social interactions. Just as a snake flicks its tongue out, catches scents, and deposits them on the roof of its mouth for analysis, sheep too can gather airborne scents, primarily those associated with sex and dominance. The animal performing the lipcurl will tilt its head up and back in a present-like posture and curl its lips back, exposing the gums. It then draws air in through its mouth, across the Jacobson's organ. Flicking its tongue in and out, it gathers additional scents from its own muzzle, "tasting" the smell. During the rut, rams will nuzzle a ewe's genitals or her urine on the ground and then lipcurl, determining whether or not she is in estrus and ready to mate. Within ram band, there is a fair amount of lipcurling associated with horning, presenting, neck fights, and lo stretches year-round, as the rams sort out dominance issues.

A dominant ram sometimes approaches a subordinate or rough equal and using one of his front legs, delivers a good solid thump, usually to the other's chest or side. This isn't a pawing motion; the whole leg is swung forward and strikes across a broad area. These *front kicks* usually follow lo stretches and present threats and represent an escalation of the interaction between two nearly equal rams. After receiving a couple of front kicks, a subordinate ram will sometimes submit to having the dominant place his head across his back or even to being mounted.

Mounting in this context is a dominance display without sexual overtones and is most often done from the rear or the side. If the ram on the receiving end of the front kick or mounting attempt feels that he is the dominant one, he will respond with a lo stretch or a present threat of his own, which may lead to a direct face-off between the two.

Both sexes use *head butts* to boot subordinates out of the way, and ewes will sometimes butt lambs that are too persistent in their efforts to nurse. During the rut, ewes who do not wish to mate will sometimes turn on pushy rams and butt them, or threaten to butt them. The full-tilt brawls that are the trademark of mountain sheep are the exclusive domain of mature rams. Two 300-pound rams pulling out all the stops and going head-to-head is a truly awesome spectacle. With a closing speed of nearly thirty miles per hour, upwards of 600 pounds of muscle and horn collide, generating over 7,800 pounds of force. Put another way, the impact is roughly equal to a ram falling on his head from a height of thirty feet. While they occur

LEFT: STONE'S SHEEP NECK FIGHTING, MUNCHO LAKE PROVINCIAL PARK, BRITISH COLUMBIA, CANADA
OPPOSITE, LEFT: BIGHORN RAM PERFORMING LIP CURL WITH LO STRETCH, GLACIER NATIONAL PARK
OPPOSITE, RIGHT: BIGHORN RAM ISSUING A FRONT KICK. JASPER NATIONAL PARK

year-round, these clashes are at their most fierce during the rut, often in direct defense of an estrous ewe. Battles can last for hours, even through the night, which can leave rams too tired to mate. Ewes coming into estrus sometimes have to take the initiative and actually butt or kick an exhausted suitor to his feet.

Mountain sheep are socially playful and innovative animals, and it is not at all uncommon to see individuals breaking or bending the "rules" of social contact to their own benefit. Depending on the particular dispositions involved, younger subordinate rams will occasionally be allowed to play the role of superior over the dominant rams in their band, but only temporarily.

During rutting season, late November and early December, the game becomes much more serious. In the presence of an estrous ewe, a dominant ram will become highly aggressive towards other rams and will initiate as many clashes as it takes to drive off competing males. During these clashes, rams not involved in the conflict often try to sneak in and mate with the ewe, or to drive her away from the rams fighting over her. Often, the ewe recognizes these rams' lower status and does not cooperate, but occasionally one will allow a lesser ram to mate with her while the dominant rams are occupied with the fight.

Seasonal exhaustion caused by rut contributes to higher overwinter mortality rates for mature dominant rams as opposed to subordinate rams and ewes. On average, once a ram reaches a position of social dominance, he has only a few years to live. The tremendous toll of the rut will catch up to him one fall and the subsequent winter will take his life. Rams maturing very rapidly, reaching their full-body and large-horn size at an early age, suffer from the "James Dean" syndrome—they live fast and die young,

rarely living longer than twelve years. Rams maturing more slowly tend to have a longer life expectancy, into their mid- to late teens.

Ewes average significantly longer lives than rams, often making it well into their teens, with some reaching their mid-twenties. This difference in life-spans is probably due to the difference in the timing of each gender's most serious physical demands. Ewes' most stressful time comes when they are birthing and then suckling young during the spring and summer, which is when food resources are at their most nutritious and abundant. They can readily find enough calories to meet their immediate needs plus enough extra for full recovery from birthing. Rams, however, face their most stressful period at a time when forage is rapidly decreasing in both quantity and nutrition. They almost certainly will not recoup the calories lost to the rut and will go into winter with greatly depleted fat reserves. Thus the most dominant rams, the individuals involved in the bulk of the contests for mating opportunities, are the ones most likely to die the following winter.

⁂ ⁂ ⁂

All of today's mountain sheep—bighorn, Dall's, and Stone's—are creatures of habit. They are conservative, even stodgy by nature, and are notoriously bad at colonizing new territory on their own. They stick to traditional migration routes and ranges; even in the face of depleted food supplies, they often will not search for new habitat.

CLASHING RAMS, JASPER NATIONAL PARK

Initially, this would seem to be at odds with their history as pioneers of the rugged, ice-covered New World. But it is not. In order for mountain sheep to physically investigate a new area, they must see or smell something that indicates that it's suitable. Without this evidence, it simply does not exist for them and they stay where they are.

The Pleistocene environment offered few barriers to such a style of colonization. It was a wide-open world where mountain ranges were separated primarily by tundra and taiga. Today, connecting ridges and valleys are often heavily forested, creating effective barriers to sheep dispersal. These barriers are breached only if they cross traditional migration paths, and even these can be lost if key individuals die before younger members learn the way. When this happens, the route and the foraging range beyond it are lost.

There is mounting evidence that these traditional routes are slowly but surely disappearing due to rising tree lines and fire-suppression policies designed to preserve forests. These policies have a negative effect on sheep habitat, as trees that would otherwise periodically burn out now have a chance to grow, closing off sheep migration corridors. Throw in human development in the form of resource extraction, housing, and recreational facilities, and the threat to the mountain sheep is clear.

There may be a time when humans are the primary, if not sole, agent of dispersal and genetic mixing. In some areas, this role has already been adopted. Recent experiments in manipulating sheep movements and reestablishing traditional migration routes met with moderate success in Colorado. Wily researchers, understanding that sex sells, transplanted mature females onto deserted sheep range. When the ewes came into heat in the fall, distant rams literally got wind of them and migrated, following the ewes' scent along a route that had not been used for generations.

Whether this route will be permanently maintained has yet to be seen, but the possibility that such elegantly simple and inexpensive tactics may work is good news for isolated populations everywhere.

Mountain sheep do extremely well when they are introduced onto suitable or historic range. The long-extinct Audubon's bighorn of the South Dakota badlands (wiped out by commercial hunting) have been replaced by modern transplants, and these are thriving. Wild Horse Island in northwest Montana's Flathead Lake harbors a flourishing population that grows so rapidly that every few years a hundred or more are available for transplant to other regions.

Mountain bighorn have been transplanted onto numerous ranges throughout Montana, Idaho, Washington, New Mexico, Colorado, South Dakota, and British Columbia. Many of these transplants have taken place over the last fifty years and were made to provide sport-hunting opportunities. While the ethics

of introducing and growing wildlife in order to kill it are debatable, these outlying "plants" may one day provide a genetic reserve that can be used to bolster beleaguered or failing wild populations. In the case of New Mexico and South Dakota, where entire native populations were gone by the early twentieth century, all of today's mountain sheep are the descendants of transplants.

Until the late nineteenth century, bighorns ranged well out onto the Great Plains. Wherever there was broken ground, badlands, mountain ranges, or river bluffs, there were bighorn. Upwards of two million occupied North America, with approximately one and a half million in the lower forty-eight alone. Then rifle-toting colonists showed up and the bighorns' traditional defensive tactic of scrambling up steep bluffs and cliffs failed them miserably. First the cliffs along river courses, the human highways of the time, then the interior mountains, were swept clean of them. In a matter of decades, creatures that had survived everything from glacial ages to saber-toothed cats were all but wiped out. Only those living in

inaccessible or hostile environments—the deserts, a very few river courses, badlands, and the highest, most remote mountains—survived. Far to the north, Dall's and Stone's sheep were largely spared these pressures faced by their southern cousins. While they placidly grazed high mountain slopes, the men below stared downward into gold pans and sluice boxes. The hordes of people frantically scratching the earth in search of gold, fueled their quest with the meat of more easily killed lowland ungulates such as moose and caribou.

Humans weren't the only hazard endured by wild sheep, however; they also faced another more insidious enemy. Domestic sheep, turned loose on ranges throughout the southern half of wild-sheep country, carried with them a host of deadly diseases and parasites. Just as the immune systems of Native Americans were not prepared to face smallpox, wild sheep were not equipped to battle new microbial enemies. And the enemy list was long: mange, scours, lumpy jaw, blue tongue, anthrax, pink eye, sore mouth or scabby mouth, lung worm, and other deadly or debilitating diseases and parasites. All were passed from domestic sheep to their wild kin, often with catastrophic results. The entire bighorn population of Montana's Bear Paw Mountains was wiped out by anthrax in the late nineteenth century. The Tarryall Mountain, Colorado, herd of 350 sheep, virtually all suffering from lung worm, was ravaged by pneumonia in the winter of 1923 and 1924; twelve survived.

These are not isolated incidents. Today, study after study shows that lung-worm infections are a normal occurrence for many (in some regions, virtually all) adult bighorns, reducing their overall vigor, resistance to diseases, and ability to overcome harsh environmental conditions. Even the national parks don't provide safe havens; deadly diseases continue to sweep through wild populations with devastating results. In the winter of 1981 and 1982, pink eye, a bacterial

infection that often results in blindness, hit the northern population of bighorn sheep in Yellowstone National Park. Well over half of the region's five hundred sheep perished. Livestock grazing near park boundaries were the suspected carriers, but the exact source of the infection was never discovered. Now, after what amounts to a hundred years of conventional and biological warfare, the total count for all wild sheep is down to around thirty thousand, or about 1.5 percent of their original, precolonial numbers.

As easily managed as they are, mountain sheep still face serious threats, primarily from disease and, to a lesser degree, habitat loss. While we successfully engage in moving sheep and establishing new populations in new or previously occupied habitats, the core of mountain sheep habitat, the Rockies and their foothills, faces a continued onslaught from mineral and livestock interests. The latter is a particular threat, as it virtually always brings disaster in the form of disease and parasites to local mountain sheep populations. However, land managers are increasingly cognizant of the dangers livestock pose to wildlife and are adjusting grazing leases accordingly. There is still a long way to go before the future of mountain sheep is secure, but we do seem to be moving in the right direction.

ABOVE: BIGHORN RAM WITH PINK EYE, JASPER NATIONAL PARK
OPPOSITE AND RIGHT: BIGHORN RAMS IN GLACIER NATIONAL PARK

Mountain Goats

No other North American animal was more distinctly carved and molded by Pleistocene ice than the mountain goat. All of the high country's other inhabitants have nearby, closely related lowland kin, but not the mountain goat. It appears to have evolved almost completely in—no, *with*—the mountains; the same forces that carved mountain cirques and sculpted ridges from enormous slabs of the earth's crust, hammered out this tough, remarkable creature. Living their lives almost exclusively among the cliffs and crags, they move calmly and methodically across the

steepest faces, yet when the need arises, can explode into a rebounding, ricocheting blur of white, finding security on the tiniest of nubs, cracks, and ledges.

They remain among the crags through the most brutal winters, negotiating ice-covered ledges and avalanche chutes as a matter of daily routine. To avoid deepening snows, they gradually move into steeper, more treacherous cliffs, even if this means spending the winter at higher elevation. In all, mountain goats do not stand in defiance of the mountain environment but rather, are part of it, living appendages of the rock.

More than a century passed before white settlers were able to sort through myths and misinformation and accept the existence of these unlikely creatures. Native people along the coast of British Columbia traded mountain goat hides to Captain James Cook in the late eighteenth century, but he did not believe (or perhaps didn't understand) their description of the animal and decided that the hides belonged to a small southern polar bear species. In 1805, Lewis and Clark arrived at a fairly precise description based on the accounts of local native people, and yet still concluded that mountain goats were either white antelope or buffalo. A few years later, in 1811, explorer Alexander Henry may have become the first white man actually to see one in what is today Kootenay National Park in Canada. As late as 1879, explorer Alexander Mackenzie reported seeing white buffalo, which were almost certainly mountain goats, near the mouth of his namesake river. Finally, by the end of the nineteenth century, sufficient sightings, hides, and trophies had been accumulated and examined to allow taxonomists to name it—*Oreamnus americanus*—and thus bring it into official existence.

Today, mountain goats are found in the Rockies and outlying ranges from Wyoming north well into Yukon, and in coastal ranges from the Cascades in

temperature is over sixty degrees Fahrenheit, and they prefer slopes steeper than forty degrees mixed with vertical or near-vertical cliffs.

The mountain goats in the Black Hills; the Olympic Peninsula; and in all of Colorado, Utah, and Nevada are there because of recent transplanting. The Olympic population has, in fact, turned out to be something of a game-management nightmare. Biologists were correct in their speculation that the peninsula would provide outstanding goat habitat, but did not anticipate the tremendous damage the animals could do to Olympic's unique and delicate plant communities. A relatively simple ecological fact was overlooked: goats had never naturally occurred on the Olympic Peninsula and many of the alpine plant communities there evolved in the absence of large grazers. The goats' constant pruning of these plants is simply too much for them and the ground cover is rapidly dying out. In recent years, repeated attempts to remove the goats by humane means such as darting and livetrapping have failed and the only remaining, albeit unsavory, option may be to hunt them out.

The immediate ancestry of modern mountain goats is a mystery. It appears that during at least the last couple of glacial ages, there were actually two very similar white climbers sharing North America's mountains: the modern species, *Oreamnus americanus*, and a smaller, more wide-ranging creature that taxonomists named *Oreamnus harringtoni*. *Harringtoni* remains have been found from British Columbia all the way down into Mexico in habitats similar to those of contemporary goats. The reasons for *harringtoni's* extinction are unknown, but all appear to have died off about ten to fifteen thousand years ago, leaving *Oreamnus americanus* alone upon the peaks. Both species appear to have evolved not from goats, but rather as part of a tribe of creatures called *rupicaprids*. Rupicaprids share some characteristics of both wild sheep and antelope, but taxonomically fit with neither. The chamois of

Washington north to Alaska's southern mountains. There are also populations in the Black Hills of South Dakota and in the mountains of Colorado, Nevada, Utah, and on Washington's Olympic Peninsula. There are occasional rumors of them being sighted as far north as Denali National Park, Alaska, but these identifications are probably incorrect reports based on glimpses of Dall's sheep ewes or young rams. It is doubtful that there are any established populations much north of the Wrangell-Saint Elias Mountains.

At the southern end of their range, goats are virtually always found near or above the tree line, whereas to the north, if steep, craggy terrain extends low enough, they will venture as low as sea level. Their vertical range is determined by a combination of temperature and topography: they will not normally go into areas where the average daily summer

Europe and the goral and serow of Asia are also rupicaprids and distant cousins of North American mountain goats. But with these far-off relatives, the evolutionary trail stops; no living intermediate forms or close relatives are known, and few remains exist to offer hints as to the goats' recent origins.

The modern-day mountain goat is a walking laundry list of ice-age adaptations. The winter coat of these stout creatures is made up of dense, fine wool overlaid by long, thick guard hairs; you could easily bury your hand up to the wrist in it. This thick coat covers everything except the face and the lower third of the legs, which are more lightly furred probably for reasons of eyesight and mobility. The winter coat is shed each spring; during this time, both male and female mountain goats look rather bedraggled, trailing rafts of tangled fur and showing almost-bare patches of gray skin. The nannies take this look well into the summer, as the demands of nursing force their bodies to delay summer coat production, and bits and pieces of the winter coat continue to hang on. Throughout the high country each spring, tufts of loose fur hang up in vegetation as the goats brush by, decorating the Krummholz like out-of-season, raggedy little Christmas trees.

The goat's overall body shape suits a world of narrow ledges. Unlike mountain sheep, which have barrel-shaped, top-heavy bodies, goats viewed from the front are flatter, wider at the base, and have a lower center of gravity. From the side, they look something like bison, with large forequarters perfectly suited for hoisting themselves up cliffs tapering to quick-pivoting, compact, strong hindquarters. This powerful body is supported by legs and hooves adapted to the life of a rock climber. Unlike the solid

Opposite and right: Mountain goats in Glacier National Park

hooves of most other ungulates, goat hooves are composites of a hard outer rim surrounding a canine-like leathery central pad. The outer edge gives the animal a surface with which to grip cracks and lips of rock and to cut into snow and ice, while the rough, soft center provides a pliable surface that molds to small irregularities and sticks to smooth rock and ice. Further, while most ungulates have fairly tight leg joints that hinge only fore and aft, goats' joints also flex laterally, allowing them to match the angle of their hooves to the angle of the terrain and maximize surface contact. These body, leg, and hoof adaptations make for a superb mountain climber but a poor runner. On flat land, mountain goats are slow compared to other ungulates and could be run down by virtually any predator. Mountain goats rely on methodical climbing, not speed, in hairy terrain to elude predators.

Their digestive systems are equally remarkable. Unlike most other grazers, which are able to handle only a narrow range of plant types, mountain goats can eat just about anything that grows, from woody shrubs, trees, and other browse through grasses, sedges, and flowering plants to mosses and lichens. Since these animals are essentially anchored to the mountains, limited to cooler, near-vertical habitats throughout their range, they must be able to survive on whatever this environment has to offer. For example, goats are often seen licking up automobile antifreeze overflow in high-altitude parking lots, apparently without negative consequences. When this was investigated, researchers discovered that ingesting this potent poison created no adverse side effects. One researcher even went so far as to speculate that an adult goat could consume upwards of a

OPPOSITE: MOUNTAIN GOAT NANNY WITH KID, GLACIER NATIONAL PARK

RIGHT: DANCING MOUNTAIN GOAT, GLACIER NATIONAL PARK

liter of antifreeze, enough to kill over a dozen dogs, with only minor consequences.

Males, or billies, average about 240 pounds, although they can weigh up to 300 pounds. Females, called nannies whether or not they have young (kids), average about 180 pounds. Both sexes have a set of black, daggerlike horns between eight and fourteen inches long. Male mountain goat horns are a little thicker at the base and begin to curve back in a smooth arc immediately out of the head. The females' horns are more slender than the males' and rise relatively straight out of the head before curving back near the tips. (As both males and females have "beards," using this trait to sex the animals is risky. At moderate distances, the best way to tell gender is by horn shape.) Dagger-sharp and powered by a heavily muscled neck and forequarters, the horns are by far the most wicked appendages carried by any high-country grazer.

Goats use their horns as defensive weapons and in aggressive interactions with their own kind. This has influenced yet another adaptation, the thickness of the hide on their haunches. Unlike mountain sheep, who engage in head-to-head combat and have evolved thick skulls, goats have frail skulls and their dominance battles are head to tail. Two goats will attempt to gore each other in twirling, whirling, head-to-hindquarters conflicts. The hide on their haunches, not including fur, is upwards of one inch thick (twenty-five millimeters). Hide elsewhere on the body ranges from only one to five millimeters.

Late each fall, usually in early- to mid-November, billies come down from their isolation in the high cliffs and frequent the fringes of the bands. Occasionally one of these billies will enter the band and carefully, very carefully, approach each of the nannies to test her urine for the smell of estrus. Even the most powerful billy approaches the nannies in a submissive posture, ready to jump aside in an instant.

A serious goring awaits any billy who annoys a nanny. Nannies are not at all receptive to the billies' advances until they are in estrus, and even then will not allow a close approach unless they are sure of their own footing. At this point, if she is willing to mate, the nanny slightly lowers her hindquarters and allows the billy to mount her.

During the rut, battles over mating rights are almost sure to erupt. When two rival billies in pursuit of the same nanny meet, they begin a slow, stiff-legged, horn-waving, head-to-rump walk around each other. If neither backs down, their circling speeds up and they parry and feint at each other's haunches. Some confrontations can escalate further to all-out, hooking, jabbing, stabbing, twirling brawls and the fur literally flies. Evenly matched contestants will rarely hurt each other, but some of these battles are incredibly lopsided. Younger, smaller, and inexperienced billies take on massive mature billies in battles that are sometimes bloody, or even fatal. In one instance, a researcher found the carcass of a young billy that had been gored over a dozen times; virtually all of its major organs were pierced.

Mismatches are not all that uncommon among mountain goats, possibly as a result of their lack of social experience. Where mountain sheep rams spend their entire lives engaged in social activities that allow them to test their status against other rams, mountain goat billies only come together briefly once a year. At this pace, it can take years for a billy to develop any kind of social judgment. Lesser billies cannot tell when they are overmatched until the battle is joined; then they are overwhelmed and it is too late. Fortunately, the more common result of these lopsided battles is a beaten-up billy who manages to escape with his hide more-or-less intact. By persisting in

DRIED BLOOD ON HAUNCHES OF A MOUNTAIN GOAT, AGGRESSOR IN FOREGROUND, GLACIER NATIONAL PARK

the face of repeated defeats, these lesser billies gain social experience, and, assuming they survive, begin breeding as early as they possibly can, when they win their first dominance bout.

Each winter, mountain goats avoid deepening snows by moving into steep cliffs, and have developed an interesting winter-feeding strategy. Although they will feed on the meager vegetation and lichens of the cliffs, they prefer the less steep terrain's more-abundant vegetation. Each morning, they leave the cliffs in search of forage, filling their bellies with readily available browse from juniper and other varieties of Krummholz, which are hard to digest and of relatively low nutritional value. They then spend the rest of the day searching out more choice and nutritious foods. In effect, they fill up on the "sure thing" and then have the luxury of being selective for the rest of the day. If a predator appears or a storm blows in and the goats have to retreat to the cliffs, they have full stomachs. Their quest for high-grade food is thus fueled with low-grade forage, conserving precious fat reserves.

In the spring, from about the last week of May to the first week of June, pregnant nannies head off by themselves into steep, secluded cliffs. Here, the nanny gives birth on a narrow ledge to a spindly-legged six-to nine-pound kid. After licking the kid clean, which stimulates its circulation and imprints her with its scent, she then eats the afterbirth. This reduces the likelihood of attracting predators and also returns to her body some of the calories and protein that she lost during gestation. Within a few hours, the kid can follow its mother short distances among the rocks. For several days, she and her kid remain in seclusion, the nanny grazing on nearby lichens and whatever other

vegetation is at hand, the kid nursing frequently and exploring the vertical world nearby. The nanny ranges progressively farther from the birthing place, and into more and more challenging terrain, the kid at her heels. In a matter of a few days, the kid is taking small leaps from nub to nub and is able to scramble after its mother through all but the toughest terrain.

During these first few days of its life, the single greatest hazard to the kid is the golden eagle, itself hunting to feed its young. While a baby mountain goat would be too heavy for all but the largest eagle to carry off, the bird can occasionally yank one off a cliff; the fall kills it and the eagle can then feed on the carcass at its leisure. The nanny's defense against these aerial predators is fairly straightforward: when she spots an eagle, she immediately places herself between her young and the outer world, pinning her kid to the mountainside with her body. Shielded behind this horned wall of white fur, the kid is untouchable.

About a week after birth, nannies lead their kids down out of seclusion in the cliffs and join bands composed of other nannies and kids. A few juveniles and those adult females who did not conceive are also part of these groups. The bands spend the summer grazing on the relatively gentle, vegetation-covered slopes near steep escape cliffs. The kids play together, graze and nurse, but most of their time is spent sleeping, often nestled in against the nannies' uphill side. These first few months of life will account for virtually all of the close physical contact a mountain goat experiences, unless it is a female and has young of its own. Mountain goats don't seem to particularly care for each other's company—or it may be that other than maternal relationships, mountain goats simply cannot afford close social interaction. Billies in particular lead solitary, ascetic lives, each tending to keep to himself among the highest cliffs for most of the year.

Overall, the life of a mountain goat is several degrees more dangerous than even that of mountain sheep. Their world of narrow ledges and treacherous, slippery terrain precludes the shoulder-to-shoulder jostling common to many herd animals. For mountain goats, closeness is a liability. So why do nannies, kids, and juveniles form a herd? The answer is probably predation. Inexperienced individuals, yearlings, and the season's kids are at risk—their lack of size, strength, and experience makes them relatively easy targets. Without the alert and multiple eyes, ears, and noses of the herd, and in some cases the protective shield of the nannies, young goats would stand little chance of survival. Even within a band, however, they don't get too close; the rule within the group seems to be "keep your distance."

Nannies shepherd their kids through the winter, leading them from foraging area to foraging area, but do not directly assist them in feeding—the kids must paw down through the snow themselves. However, if a kid has found a good feeding spot and an adolescent or other adult tries to displace it, the nanny fiercely defends her kid and its little patch of ground.

Winter is by far the hardest season for all mountain goats, and avalanches and slips off icy cliffs claim many. In years of extreme cold combined with deep snows, the young in particular suffer. Relegated to areas already pawed out and picked over by adults, they usually find little forage left. Combined with the increased caloric demands of extreme cold, mortality among juveniles can soar to nearly one hundred percent. Yet if a kid makes it past its first year, its chances of survival improve dramatically and it may live into its early teens.

❊   ❊   ❊

It is thought that at the turn of the century, the mountain goat population numbered well over one hundred fifty thousand; today, there are no more than thirty thousand. From the early 1900s well into the 1970s, sport hunting took a tremendous toll on goat populations, particularly throughout the Rockies. Alberta, on the eastern front of the Rockies, was heavily populated with mountain goats in 1909. Then sport hunting was initiated by the provincial government, and by 1970, it was closed to hunting due to a lack of goats. The populations still haven't recovered.

Game managers didn't understand basic goat biology and were applying hunting quotas, based on deer models, to goats. In nature, all age classes of deer suffer similar, moderate rates of mortality, and there are lots of subadults shouldering their way into the adult population. With goats, juvenile mortality is extremely high while adult mortality is comparatively low. While hunter-caused mortality in adult deer is easily compensated for by plenty of younger animals, in the world of the mountain goat, there are barely enough juveniles to replace adults lost to natural causes. Since hunters take adults, they radically increase mortality in an age class that normally has a low mortality rate, and the effect is twofold: kids lose their mothers to hunters and don't survive the winter, increasing already-high juvenile mortality numbers; and the population of adults goes down. Heavily hunted populations spiral downward to zero with frightening speed. In a nutshell, nature's accounting system for mountain goats is so tight that there are very few "excess" goats for human hunters to take. Fortunately, knowledge of goat biology surged ahead of hunting pressure through the 1960s and 1970s and much more conservative hunting quotas were established throughout the U.S. and Canada. Today, mountain goat populations are fairly stable throughout their range, but it was a close call.

Mountain goat kid in winter coat, Glacier National Park

Mountain Caribou

A small herd of caribou breaks from the timber. Eyes wide, nostrils twitching, heads high, they quickly slalom up through the Krummholz and onto the tundra, where their strides lengthen and they smoothly pick up speed. Occasionally, one of them stops to nibble at something on the ground or to bite at its own flanks fiercely, leaving bits of hair fluttering on the wind. Then, seeing that he has fallen behind the band, the straggler hurries to catch up, effortlessly closing the gap with huge, gangly strides. The animals click softly with each step as the loose bones and elastic tendons supporting their oversized hooves splay and flex, absorbing the irregularities of the soggy tundra. A sound like dozens of dice being shaken in a cloth pouch accompanies the band wherever it goes.

They are ascending to avoid a plague of insects in the timber where they spent much of the night feeding. As the sun warms the trees, hordes of deer flies, bot flies, black flies, and mosquitoes become active and converge on the small band, turning the caribou into a mass of scratching, snorting, twitching gray fur.

They course upward across the tundra, maintaining their pace until they reach talus at the base of a long, steep slope capped by a snowfield. Here, they slow considerably and begin to pick their way up through the rocks, looking comically nearsighted as they carefully inspect each bit of ground for stability. After ascending the talus, they head immediately to the snowbank. Several lay down, pushing their noses against the snow. Some paw out small depressions and then put their noses down in them. This strange behavior is due primarily to a plain-looking but particularly nasty little fly called a bot.

Some species of bot flies lay their eggs inside the noses of ungulates. Once they hatch, the larvae burrow up into tissues surrounding the sinus cavities and skull, where they feed and mature. Then they find their way through the sinuses to the back of the throat and are coughed up by the hapless host. This activity is irritating to the caribou and drives them to seek relief in the snow. The cold, combined with high winds on the exposed snowbank, keeps these and other insects at bay. But it only slows, and doesn't stop, the persistent hordes. Soon there is a cloud of biting flies around the band and they are again scratching and snorting.

Suddenly, as if on cue, the whole band is on its feet again. Shaking, snorting, and stomping, they break into a gallop, leaving most of the insects behind. At the other end of the snowfield, they stop and some once again lie down while others dig holes for their noses. The band will spend the entire day repeating this scene, running from one end of the snowfield to the other about once every half hour.

They will not feed until the cool of night forces the insects into dormancy.

A handful of these isolated herds wander the mountains from the Idaho Panhandle north to Jasper National Park, Canada. Very little is known of these nomadic "mountain" caribou. Throughout their range, they are often little more than rumors: a hoof print in the mud, a glimpse on a ridge, a gnawed antler or clump of fur left over from a wolf kill. Some say that they are just groups of woodland caribou that happen to live in the mountains, while others feel they warrant subspecies status. Still others, a fast-growing majority, say that they are an ecotype of woodlands, a race complete with behaviors and traditions all their own.

This confusion as to what a mountain caribou actually is has led to some serious problems for researchers in the field. One long-term study in the Jasper National Park area may have included an entire population that was not mountain caribou at all but rather, "regular" woodlands. Even their total range and numbers are disputed. Recent anecdotal evidence has them expanding their range into the mountains south of Glacier National Park, Montana, while population estimates fall anywhere between one and three thousand, depending on who's doing the counting.

The confusion as to where mountain caribou fit within the caribou family is part of an even larger controversy as to how, or even whether, to divide caribou into separate species or subspecies at all. Traditional biology divides North American caribou into two species, the barren-ground and woodland. Barren-ground live primarily in or near the Arctic and are the ones so well-known for their migratory life style. Huge herds of barren-ground caribou cover tremendous distances each spring and fall as they cross vast

MOUNTAIN CARIBOU COURSING, JASPER NATIONAL PARK

expanses of tundra and taiga, traveling to and from traditional calving grounds. Woodland, on the other hand, lead much more stationary lives; they are usually found south of the Arctic Circle, scattered throughout the boreal and temperate forests of the north, ranging as far south as the Idaho Panhandle and as far east as Nova Scotia.

Recent genetic sampling has revealed some interesting information about these animals, information that butts squarely up against accepted wisdom of clearly defined caribou species. It appears that all caribou are part of one long genetic gradation; barren-ground contain woodland genes and vice-versa. Starting in Alaska's arctic, and moving south and east, barren-ground genes are replaced by an ever-increasing proportion of woodland genes. This gradation makes it very difficult, perhaps even wrong, to separate them into different species. It may be more appropriate to divide them up into ecotypes of one species, as is currently the case with mountain caribou.

So where does that leave our wandering tribes of mountain caribou? We may never really know. The population in the Jasper National Park area is in the midst of a free-fall, their numbers plummeting from fifteen hundred or more in the early 1960s to only a few hundred today. Some populations in interior British Columbia appear to be faring a little better, but with current logging quotas expanding throughout their range, their future is also in question. Unfortunately, information needed to make sound environmental decisions regarding mountain caribou is in short supply.

This has Canadian and, to a lesser degree, American researchers scrambling to answer fundamental behavioral, genetic, and ecological questions: what

MOUNTAIN CARIBOU, JASPER NATIONAL PARK, CANADA

are these creatures and where do they fall in the genetic gradation of caribou? What factors influence juvenile and adult mortality? Do clearcuts and other human disturbances within caribou range influence migration patterns? If so, is there a way of mitigating these influences? Why have some populations nosedived while others in similar habitats appear to be stable? In the face of what seems to be an overall decline in population numbers, why are sightings becoming more widespread? Are dispersing animals fleeing some sort of ecological pressure and searching for new, suitable habitats? And from which populations are these dispersers originating? These and other questions are the subjects of current research and will probably be answered soon.

For now, we have the basics. Mountain caribou differ significantly from typical woodlands caribou in their local migration patterns. Where woodlands normally remain in timbered habitat year-round, mountain caribou migrate vertically, in and out of timbered areas, depending on season and snow conditions. A typical yearly cycle for mountain caribou would be as follows: Fall rut, from September to mid-November (the longest rutting period for any of the high country's ungulates), is spent at high altitudes, either at or above tree line. Late fall to early winter, they descend to below tree line, avoiding winter's first onslaughts and seeking out stands of mature timber that can supply them with arboreal lichens; these lichens are a critical caribou winter food source and are found in quantity only in mature forests. Mid- to late winter, they ascend above tree line to windswept areas, escaping the deep soft snows and predators of the drifted-in valleys. Late winter to early spring, they descend below tree line to take advantage of the hard-packed snow that will now support their weight, allowing them to feed on lichen higher in the trees. As calving approaches, around the end of May, they migrate once again to high altitudes, fleeing predators and insects, and spend the balance of the summer there.

This general overview does not account for all mountain caribou migration patterns. Some bands have a bias toward higher- or lower-altitude regions, or simply migrate up in the spring and down in the late fall. Each band establishes its own pattern. Regardless of individual preferences, however, all mountain caribou appear to be tied to mountainous terrain, specifically regions with mature stands of timber below and alpine tundra above.

Unlike other North American members of the deer family, in which only the males have antlers, caribou of both sexes grow antlers, but at different times of year. Male antler growth begins in the early spring and can be as fast as a half an inch a day. The antlers reach full size late in the summer, just before rut, and are then shed in the early winter. Female antler growth begins in late summer and matures in the winter, to be shed in the spring. The difference in the timing of this growth hints at different purposes for male and female headgear. The primary use for male antlers is fairly obvious: as weapons and status symbols. Female antlers are probably also used to compete with rival males, but the object of the competition is food rather than reproduction. Caribou live in very harsh environments and, unlike other deer that remain segregated and widely dispersed in winter, the sexes stay together in large bands throughout the season. Female caribou need some way of leveling the playing field in the competition with males for scarce winter food. The fact that females have antlers in the heart of winter while the males are antlerless gives the females, particularly those with developing fetuses, an advantage over the larger males when it comes to defending or usurping desirable forage.

Each fall, beginning around mid-September, mountain caribou begin congregating on high open patches of tundra, signaling the onset of rut. Caribou are polygamous, with the largest and most dominant males gathering harems of females and defending them from rival males much like their distant lowland cousins, the elk. Large bulls duel head-to-head for possession of these harems, and although the battles are hard-fought, serious injuries are rare. As with most ungulates, the rut is a taxing time for dominant male caribou, which spend the majority of their time herding females and driving off rival males at the expense of feeding. They can lose up to twenty percent of their body weight and go into winter greatly weakened; this is reflected in mortality figures for males, who typically don't live much beyond age eight. Like mountain sheep, they die near their peak of social dominance.

A typical mature bull weighs from 280 to 380 pounds, and cows, around 200 to 250 pounds. Both males and females can live to a maximum of about fifteen in the wild, although as mentioned, males average closer to eight and females, twelve. Males are thought not to breed until they are at least four years old. Before then, their bodies and antlers are too small for them to be able to compete with dominant bulls. Females probably breed in their second fall, and every year until they die. Most studies have found that virtually every breeding-age female is pregnant every spring. Calf mortality is fairly high through their first summer; one study found a less than thirty percent calf-survival rate going into the first winter.

Mountain caribou, Jasper National Park, Canada

The exact causes of these high juvenile mortality rates aren't known, but one factor may be predation. Grizzly bears and wolverines frequent the same high-altitude areas caribou use for calving, and studies in the Columbia range have shown both of these carnivores to be effective predators of caribou. Wolves have frequently been blamed for early-season calf mortality, but the best evidence is that while mountain caribou are spending their springs and summers at high altitudes, wolves are down in the valleys pursuing elk, moose, deer, and their young. Wolves only occasionally make high-country hunting forays, and when they do, they are usually pursuing mountain sheep.

‡   ‡   ‡

Mountain caribou are an extremely difficult animal for game managers to manipulate or accommodate. Unlike most other members of the deer family, they range vertically through a wide variety of habitats, from valleys filled with dense, mature timber to high alpine tundra. It appears that if any part of their range is compromised, mountain caribou disappear from the area. Clearcuts in their low-altitude winter range deprives them of cover and their favored winter food, arboreal lichens. Selective cuts that leave islands of trees concentrate caribou unnaturally in these areas and make it easier for predators to key in on them. Roads leading into high- or low-altitude areas, particularly roads kept plowed in the winter, provide unnaturally easy access for predators, most notably wolves. A study found nearly three-quarters of winter wolf kills occurred near plowed roads. The livestock used by well-intentioned outfitters and backpackers carry a host of lowland parasites into the high country each year, which may be infecting caribou and adding to an already-high parasite load. Finally, human recreational developments in or near critical calving areas can lead to the animals using less-ideal areas to bear their young, which contributes to higher-than-normal calf mortality.

Despite all of this, there is reason to be cautiously optimistic about the future of the mountain caribou. With the first few tidbits of knowledge about these animals has come alarm and action. Under pressure from environmental groups and on the advice of park biologists, the superintendent of Canada's Jasper National Park closed sections of the park's northwest border. This helped reduce disturbances in critical calving and rutting areas. He also turned down a proposed recreational development in a major caribou wintering area in the Maligne Valley. Elsewhere, researchers and game managers in Canada's Glacier-Revelstoke area are scrambling to discover the answers to basic biological and ecological questions about the animals. The early data contains some good news: specific populations in the Columbia range appear to be stable. In the lower forty-eight, the idea of reintroducing mountain caribou into Glacier National Park is slowly gaining momentum and may even happen naturally, as indicated by an increasing number of sightings in the region. With a little luck, knowledge of these enigmatic creatures will continue to grow rapidly. If it does, the decline in their populations can be arrested, as it has been with the mountain goat and mountain sheep. Mountain caribou may follow the wolf south and one day be coursing along the ridges of Glacier National Park, Montana, or making pests of themselves in Banff.

Mountain lion, northwestern Montana

THE
THREAT
FROM BELOW

THE THREAT FROM BELOW

There is a group of animals that does not live permanently above the tree line, yet the mere possibility of its presence dominates the daily lives of all other high country inhabitants. They are the carnivores, and to ignore them is to become part of them. The fate of the weak, inept or careless is death by fang or talon and reincarnation as a golden eagle chick or a grizzly bear cub.

Predator versus prey is a war that never ends. It's not a war of daily head-to-head combat, claw against horn, but rather a sensory war. The winner or loser is most often determined, long before the final pounce or chase, by the keenness of the senses and the alertness or experience of the minds.

Prey animals sport an impressive array of long-range sensory organs capable of detecting all but the most stealthy approaches. Their eyes are sharp and positioned near the sides of their heads, giving them nearly 360-degree vision. Their cup-shaped ears pivot, sweeping the environment and pinpointing the slightest rustle. Even a few molecules of wolf floating on the wind are picked up by sensitive nostrils and an alarm is raised. Combined, these senses form a defensive dome around the animal, an area constantly swept for information, within which almost all other animals are detected.

Facing this dome is the predator. Its goal is to bore a hole through the dome and create a tunnel leading to its prey. All the while, the senses of prey animals are sweeping over and around it, reaching out for the first faint clues of its presence.

Carnivores need meat. With the notable exception of the bears, all of the high-country predators must consume flesh to survive. Their diges-tive systems, right down to the flora and fauna living in their guts, can only process preassembled proteins. They can digest vegetable fats and carbohydrates fairly well, but with nowhere near the efficiency needed to survive on plants alone.

Carnivores are equipped with two very efficient types of teeth: *canines* and *carnassials*. The canines, or fangs, are the most obvious. Large, sharp, paired pegs at the fronts of both the lower and upper jaws, these teeth are primarily for piercing and gripping. They are the tools with which carnivores grab and drag down their prey; once these teeth are firmly embedded, the prey's fate is almost always sealed. Carnassials, the massive crushing and shearing teeth, are a predator's silverware: the tools of feeding, not killing. Carnassials function much the same way as pinking shears. When a carnivore clamps down with these teeth, the multiple shearing surfaces cut at several angles simultaneously. Bones and flesh are easily rent by these formidable teeth.

Backing this armament are powerful sets of muscles that wrap all the way up around the carnivore's head, attaching along the sagittal crest at the top of the skull. These muscles work in only one direction, to close the jaws, and they do this with incredible force.

IF YOU OWN A DOG, YOU MAY BE SAYING, "NOW WAIT A MINUTE, MY DOG'S DRY DOG FOOD IS ALL VEGETABLE MATTER AND SHE'S NOT STARVING. WHAT GIVES?" WHAT GIVES IS THE CLEVERNESS OF OUR SPECIES. BY SEPARATING VEGETABLE PROTEINS FROM THE SURROUNDING INDIGESTIBLE PLANT MATERIAL AND RECOMBINING A SELECTED VARIETY OF VEGETABLE COMPONENTS, PET-FOOD MANUFACTURERS ARE ESSENTIALLY ABLE TO BUILD A MEAT SUBSTITUTE STRAIGHT FROM PLANTS. WHILE HUMAN ENGINEERS CAN MAKE THIS JUMP, NATURE CAN NOT. IN THE NATURAL WORLD, THE UNFORTUNATE INTERMEDIARY BETWEEN PLANT AND CARNIVORE IS THE HERBIVORE.

TIMBER WOLF, DENALI NATIONAL PARK

An adult man could easily hold an adult wolf's mouth closed with one hand, but those same wolf jaws could shear through the man's forearm with a single bite.

Carnivores cover large areas searching for vulnerable prey, carrion, or a lucky break. By hunting across a large area, they increase their chances of encountering unwary prey. If they were to confine their hunts to a small area, prey species would simply leave or become so attuned to the individual predator's ways and daily schedule that the odds of a successful hunt would be extremely low. So they wander widely, which reduces their presence from a certainty to a possibility and encourages complacency in prey species.

The topic of wandering brings up the difference between a *home range* and a *territory*. A territory is an area marked by scents, and sometimes vocalizations, that is actively patrolled and defended. The maintenance and defense of a territory can be very elaborate and taxing, involving frequent border patrols and skirmishes, some of which can explode to all-out war. Home ranges, on the other hand, are usually defined as the total area an animal uses in the course of its daily life. Home ranges are usually scent-marked, but not defended. An individual carnivore hunting in a particular area leaves frequent scent marks around, saying, in effect, "I'm here for now and I've got dibs on this area." After the hunter leaves, others are free to move in and temporarily claim the area as their hunting ground.

Species with home ranges rather than territories avoid conflicts with each other by not being in the same place at the same time. While they will defend the area around a den or kill, most predators do not defend their total range. It is much easier for them to wander a home range and just stay out of each other's way than to risk conflicts with opponents as deadly as themselves.

Most predators large enough to draw human attention have been persecuted throughout their ranges. From the early twentieth century, well into the 1960s, both the U.S. and Canada engaged in massive predator control campaigns, which involved trapping, gassing dens, and poisoning. The U.S. was particularly successful in its campaign against the wolf. First the eastern timber wolf, then the massive buffalo wolves that roamed the Great Plains, and finally the wolves of the Mountain West fell to the poisons and snares. The death toll was enormous, conservatively numbering in the hundreds of thousands. Tallying up wolf deaths only begins to describe the carnage. Deadly poison bait stations were indiscriminate and many other predators and scavengers were decimated as well. Tiny shrews, bobcats, lynx, golden and bald eagles, ravens, turkey vultures, California condors, crows, foxes, mountain lions, badgers, coyotes, hawks, grizzly and black bears, weasels and wolverines: they were all viewed as little more than weeds, expendable in our sterilization of the west.

The Weasels

Two species of weasel frequent the mountains above tree line: the diminutive long-tail, and the beast of legends, the wolverine. Like most weasels, both species have elongated bodies, relatively short legs, and voracious appetites. The long-tail looks like a typical little weasel: sinuous, eight to ten inches long, a three- to four-inch-long tail, bright dark eyes, and weighing about half a pound. By comparison, the wolverine is a massive brute: powerfully built, two to three feet long, a bushy six-inch-plus tail, and large feet with pronounced claws. Wolverines average about thirty pounds and some reach as high as sixty. Despite its beefy build, it still has a distinct "weasely" look—long, low and quick. Early taxonomists, confused by the wolverine's massive, almost bearlike appearance, misnamed it *Ursus gulo*. *Gulo* means glutton, in reference to the beast's legendary appetite, and Ursus is the genus to which North American bears belong.

Both weasels have a physiological adaptation that is also found in bears, seals, and whales, called *delayed implantation*. After fertilization, the eggs inside the female go into a state of suspended animation within her oviduct; they do not descend into the uterus and bind, or implant, on the uterus wall. Here, the eggs can remain dormant for several months without damage. This is a very powerful survival tool for the mother. If, when the time comes for the eggs to descend and begin development, she is severely stressed—starving, sick, or injured—some or all of the eggs will automatically be aborted. Delayed implantation allows the female's body to do a sort of environmental assessment before she is burdened with a pregnancy, which increases her chances of survival.

The long-tail is a generalist, able to make a living in just about any North American environment, from Mexico north throughout the continental U.S. and well into Canada. At the northern end of their range, they molt into a beautiful white pelage in late fall, whereas at the southern end, they remain rusty brown year-round. Like most small weasels, long-tails are prolific breeders, and in warm climates may have more than one litter a year. In the mountains, particularly in the north, they are generally limited to a single litter in the spring. Young weasels mature unbelievably fast; by the time they are only a couple of weeks old, their reproductive tracts mature and the female kits sometimes go into estrus and are able to mate. Researchers have found fertilized eggs inside young females that were still nursing, a wandering male having entered the den and mated with them.

LONG-TAILED WEASEL, JASPER NATIONAL PARK

While the larger, more intimidating wolverine with its incredible strength and appetite has dominated the human imagination, the smaller long-tail is actually a far more impressive killer. On a daily basis, long-tails stalk and kill healthy prey well over ten times their size. They are half-pound eating machines driven by a hot-burning metabolism that rarely lets them rest. In cold weather, they must kill and feed at least once a day to keep their tiny bodies warm. At high altitudes they regularly hunt pika, ptarmigan, and ground squirrels, while at lower altitudes mice, rats, rabbits, hares, grouse, and poultry are on the menu.

Wolverines are not nearly so cosmopolitan. True animals of the wilderness, a few are left in the Colorado Rockies and the Sierra, but they are not found in any numbers until one reaches the wilds of northern Montana, Canada, and Alaska. Early taxonomists split Old- and New-World wolverines into two separate species, *Gulo gulo* and *Gulo luscus*, respectively. Most biologists now view them as the same species, *Gulo gulo*. In Europe, their range stretches across the northern tier of Scandinavia through to Siberia. Throughout their range, they are surrounded by myths:

> *In the arctic North of our world lives an odd animal, known as the wolverine or glutton. It is not much bigger than a full grown fox, but has the strength of a bear. It usually moves along at a rather clumsy gallop, but the best of northern long-distance skiers cannot overtake it. The wolverine can't stalk its prey noiselessly; it can't lie patiently in wait; and it can't overtake its victim by superior speed. And yet it is never short of food. Its sight is not particularly keen, nor is its hearing or sense of smell; and yet even the most skillful and experienced hunter is rarely able to bag it. It gobbles up all kinds of food voraciously, but even strong doses of strychnine cannot kill it. The highest price of any beast of prey in the Far North has been placed on its head, and yet its numbers have hardly decreased. (Peter Krott, Demon of the North)*

As with most elusive predators, the wolverine is surrounded by inaccurate lore. Like most carnivores, they have an excellent sense of smell; radio-collared individuals will make a beeline for researchers' bait stations from over two miles away. They are, like most mammals, vulnerable to strychnine, the ingestion of even small amounts being fatal. The wolverine's sensitive nose has probably contributed to the legends about their eating poisoned baits and surviving. Their keen sense of smell would make it possible for them to avoid areas of the bait tainted with poison while consuming or dragging off the rest of the carcass.

In the high country they occasionally take mountain caribou; mountain goat kids; and bighorn, Dall's or Stone's lambs, but overall their diet tends to be dominated by small mammals, birds, and carrion. Mainly it's carrion, and they don't care where they get it: trappers' traps will do just fine. Wolverines eating animals caught in traps hasn't won them any popularity points with trappers. The Cree name for the beast, *Ommeethatsees*, "one who steals," pegs the animal pretty well; he is first and foremost a consummate scavenger.

Tales of wolverine taking down reindeer in Scandinavia were largely discounted by most North American biologists since none of their early long-term studies found any evidence of them actually killing large, healthy, free-ranging prey. However, two separate studies collided recently in the Columbia Mountains of British Columbia, one on wolverines, and the other on mountain caribou. A radio-collared, thirty-pound male wolverine single-handedly took down a healthy adult male caribou. This was not what you would call a clean kill—over a period of about four days, the wolverine repeatedly attacked and injured the caribou until, weakened by the non-stop pursuit, blood loss, and shock, it was at last finished off. In a separate incident, a different, uncollared wolverine, used similar tactics to kill a radio-collared adult female caribou. While it's not likely that these incidents are commonplace, they do illustrate that at least some of the stories about wolverine ferocity are true.

In addition to the guerrilla tactics wolverines sometimes use on caribou, researchers have discovered another hunting technique that appears to be unique to the beast. In the winter, radio-collared wolverines frequently made extended forays well above tree line. This was initially something of a mystery since prey and carrion were apparently so much more abundant in the valleys. To wander up out of the sheltered, food-rich valleys and into the cold, sterile heights just didn't make sense. The surprising explanation for this behavior came from analyzing the beasts' droppings: hoary marmots. That's right, marmots in the winter. Scat analysis showed that marmots comprised upwards of ten percent of some wolverines' winter diets. They were locating dens, probably by smell, then tunneling down through several feet, or even yards, of snow and entering the hibernacula. Since marmots hibernate in a group, these dens represented a bonanza of fresh food for the wolverines.

Early studies on wolverine ecology seriously overestimated their numbers. Without the benefit of modern radio collars, researchers assumed that widely separated sets of tracks were made by different individuals. In many cases they were wrong. An individual may wander through a home range of over four hundred square miles and be on the move for up to twenty hours a day. As they found tracks in one drainage after another, researchers tallied up individual after individual, without realizing that they were smack in the middle of a single wolverine's home range. This helps explain another of the early myths

about wolverine numbers: wolverines were thought to be virtually impossible to eradicate. No matter how many people settled in an area and trapped or poisoned the beasts, hunters still saw their tracks all over the place. In reality, wolverine numbers were indeed plummeting. As human hunters depleted local game populations, the few remaining wolverines were forced to wander ever more widely to find food, leaving their tracks over a constantly increasing area.

Female wolverines can go into estrus any time from May through August, and it lasts for about one week. There is some evidence that ovulation is induced by the presence of a male; that is, the female walks around on the brink of going into heat and when a male shows up, he somehow triggers full-on estrus. This makes a lot of sense for such a wide-ranging species. If a female were to go into heat without a male nearby, her cycle could easily pass before a distant male was able to find her.

A courting pair stays together for less than a week, wandering around and feeding together. This is not an elaborate courtship—they spend time together, occasionally tussle, and then mate. If the female goes into the winter in good condition, she will select a den, usually a cave or burrow, and give birth to one to three kits in February or March.

The young grow rapidly and are weaned in about two and a half months. By the time the kits are three months old, the family will have left the den and adopted typical wolverine ways, living on the move. When the kits are eight months old, they are nearly adult-sized, with appetites to match. Fortunately for the female, they are by now becoming competent hunters and scavengers and aren't totally dependent upon her for food. At twelve to fourteen months the family begins to break up, the kits usually taking off

WOLVERINE, NORTHWEST MONTANA

together to hunt. Eventually, they also split up and go on to live solitary lives.

The wolverine's life is not easy. Many studies show overwinter adult mortality rates pushing fifty percent, the primary cause of death being "harvest": trapping. One study found that virtually every adult in the study area was missing toes and had foot or leg injuries consistent with steel leg-hold traps. This is not a pleasant way to die. The fact that these animals will rip or gnaw off their own toes is a testament to the overwhelming fear and pain they feel while in the grip of these traps. Wolverine fur is not particularly elegant nor soft; in fact, the long, stout guard hairs make it coarse by most standards. So why are they trapped? For parka hoods. Wolverine fur tends to resist frost better than other materials when drawn tight around the face. For the convenience of not having to brush off frost from the rim of a parka hood, these walking legends are killed.

Mountain Lion

Mountain Lions are the most wide-ranging and versatile of the New-World cats. Today, they can be found from southern South America north to Canada's Yukon-British Columbia border. Throughout this range they inhabit large tracts of wild lands: mountains, swamps, deciduous or coniferous forests, savannas, even tropical rain forests provide a home for these formidable predators. In the U.S. and Canada, Mountain lions once roamed coast to coast, but a penchant for horse meat and other livestock put them on early settlers' hit lists. With the exception of a small Florida Everglades population (which may be so inbred that they are already genetically extinct), they are currently found primarily in the Mountain

MOUNTAIN LION, NORTHWEST MONTANA

West. Elsewhere in the east, lions are only a rumor. Like most predators, they have not fared well against humans, although a surprising number survived the poisoning campaigns of the mid-1900s. Many were probably spared due to their finicky feline palates and preference for fresh meat; the poison-laced carcasses littering the west held little appeal.

The largest male lions can top 250 pounds, and the females 180 pounds. Both sexes hunt through home ranges of five to thirty-five square miles. While deer dominate their diet, there is no North American prey animal, except possibly an adult bison, that a healthy adult lion cannot kill. Mountain lions typically attack their prey from above, springing onto the victim's back from a ledge or tree. The cat then latches onto the prey with all four sets of claws and bites down on the base of the skull. For most victims, death is nearly instant. In some cases, if the cat is unable to penetrate dense fur or muscle at the back of the head, it will reach under the prey's neck with a forepaw and either rake the throat with its claws, or wrench the head back, breaking the neck.

Lions make exception to this hunting method when they take on mountain goats. Landing on the back of a goat, a lion would find itself staring right at those daggerlike horns. Instead, lions often attack mountain goats head-on, attempting to knock them off their feet with the sweep of a forepaw and then clamping their jaws on the underside of the goat's throat. These attacks resemble desperate fencing matches, with each participant parrying and thrusting. The goat's wicked horns and agility among the rocks are matched by the awesome speed and armament of the lion.

Female lions can breed any time of year, although they have a bias towards late winter. In the few weeks before their estrous cycle, females give off a scent attractive to males, or toms, and any in nearby home ranges will be drawn to her. Since lions have well-defined home ranges, most individuals within a region are familiar with each other. If a dominant tom shows up near a female in heat, lesser males will give way without a fight since they already know who's boss. Sometimes, however, fights occur and are serious enough that virtually all older toms carry battle scars. Once a male has established his right to a female, the pair stays together for up to two weeks. They will hunt, feed, and play together, these brief periods of courting accounting for virtually all of an adult lion's social life. By the end of the first week of courtship, the female will enter fully into estrus. This will last for seven to ten days, and the pair may mate several times a day. As the female's cycle passes, so does the tom's interest in her, and the couple separates and resumes their solitary lifestyles.

Ninety days later, generally in a cave or pile of deadfall timber, the female gives birth to one to six, blind, spotted, one-pound kittens. At about ten days, the kittens open their eyes. Initially, the mother does not leave the den but is finally driven by hunger to hunt nearby. While the kittens are in the den, she limits her range to a small area—two to five square miles. These first few months are often hard on the female, the caloric demands of nursing exacerbated by a limited hunting range. By the time the kittens reach two months, they weigh about ten pounds, are eating small amounts of meat, and are venturing out of the den with their mother on short forays. When the kittens are eight months old, their weight has increased fifty-fold over birth and they are losing their spots and accompanying their mother on hunts. As the kittens are able to forage farther and farther afield with her, the mother incrementally expands her hunting range.

The young will not actually participate in taking down big game until they are a year or more old.

When the kittens are between one and two years old, the female occasionally wounds prey but doesn't kill it, allowing the kittens to deliver the final blow. When the kittens are roughly two years old, the family breaks up. The female simply walks away from a kill and the kittens choose to stay behind.

⸶　⸶　⸶

Even with the advantage of long-range weapons, humans have a hard time hunting lions. Where grazers must be tuned-in to finding browse and other vegetation, devoting part of their senses to plant life, predators virtually always concentrate on animal life. This makes seeing them, let alone approaching them, extremely difficult and has led to hunters teaming up with another species to hunt lions: dogs. Hunting lions with hounds has become a popular sport throughout the West. The hunter usually cruises back roads with a four-wheel drive, either looking for fresh lion tracks, or with one of his dogs on the hood or roof trying to catch the scent of a cat.

When they encounter fresh sign, the dogs, often wearing radio collars in case they get lost, are released to give chase, the hunter bringing up the rear. Lions are not endurance runners, but dogs are. Usually after a chase of a few miles, the winded lion takes refuge in a tree or on a ledge, the dogs baying for all they're worth from below. The hunter eventually catches up to the melee and does one of three things: finds the lion desirable as a trophy and shoots it; finds the lion undesirable as a trophy and leaves; or takes the lion's picture and leaves.

More and more hunters are choosing the last option these days, realizing that while they themselves are predators, the kill itself is a let-down. There is something almost pathetic about the execution-style

MOUNTAIN LION, NORTHWEST MONTANA

killing of a helpless lion in a tree. The challenge, the ritual, the hunt, the need to pursue: all are fulfilled when the hunter and the dogs have successfully treed the cat. This type of catch-and-release hunting also serves a purpose. As recent deaths and attacks in Montana and California have shown, lions are dangerous to humans. Hunting, whether for trophies or photographs, serves to remind lions that we are a dangerous and unpleasant species to be around and that we are to be avoided—or at least not eaten.

Wolf

Wolves roam the wild country from Yellowstone north through Alaska. Although they are predominantly valley dwellers, they make frequent hunting forays above the tree line, taking mountain goats, mountain sheep, and mountain caribou as prey. As individuals, wolves are impressive predators: they can weigh as much as 150 pounds, lope forty miles in a single day, and exert three-quarters of a ton of shearing and crushing pressure with their massive jaws, and they have a top speed of forty miles per hour. More impressive is the wolf pack, coursing single file through the wilderness in search of prey. Excluding humans, it is the most awesome killing machine ever to roam the continent. Even the grizzly cannot stand before a determined pack.

Yet amazingly, this furry mass of golden eyes, jaws, and hunger has never once in the recorded history of North America taken humans as prey. Never. Individual wolves have attacked humans on a handful of occasions, but most of these resulted in no more than the need for a change of underwear, and none resulted in deaths. This has led some researchers to believe that humans and modern wolves may have coevolved in an environment of out-and-out cooperation. Some have gone so far as to suggest that

humans and wolves once ran together, hunting in mixed-species packs. This isn't so far-fetched, modern humans hunt with the aid of canines all the time. Why not our Pleistocene ancestors?

The basic wolf social unit is a mated pair, and together they are the beginnings of a pack. Packs have been reported to have as many as forty individuals, but five to ten is the norm. Usually, a pack consists of one mated pair, their pups from a previous year, brothers or sisters of the mated pair, and a few unrelated recruits. Normally, wolves breed in February, with only the dominant, or alpha, male and female mating in each pack. The dominant couple, through direct aggression, prevents lower-ranking individuals from mating. Gestation is about two months, and a typical litter has five blind, half- to one-pound pups. In areas where game is plentiful and aggression within the pack is low, two pairs may breed, and the females may even share the same den and suckle one another's pups. For the first four to seven weeks, the mother does not leave the den area and is entirely dependent on food brought back to her by the rest of the pack.

After about two weeks, the pups open their eyes; at approximately three or four weeks, they begin exploring the area around the mouth of the den. At six to eight weeks the pups are weaned, and they too are dependent upon the pack for food. Although the pack members will occasionally carry pieces of flesh in their mouths, they mainly carry it in their stomachs, regurgitating it on demand when the mother and the pups nip at their lips. When the pups are about two months old, their mother begins occasionally to go on hunts with the rest of the pack, leaving her pups in the care of a "baby-sitter," usually one of the lower-ranking pack members.

OPPOSITE: ALPHA FEMALE WOLF KEEPING A SUBORDINATE IN LINE, NORTHWEST MONTANA
RIGHT: WOLF IN THE HIGH COUNTRY, NORTHWEST MONTANA

When the pups are two to three months old, the family moves away from the den to a one-quarter to one-acre area called a rendezvous site. Here, the pups are left alone to hunt insects, play, and explore, while the adults go off to hunt. The adults will now be carrying back chunks of meat and hide for the pups, as well as providing regurgitated food.

They use the rendezvous site for a couple of months, until mid-fall, when the pups are big enough to come along on hunts. At first, the pups will not be much help—researchers have reported seeing them turning tail and running away at their first encounters with big game animals. But soon they're bringing up the rear and actually helping to take down prey. By the time the pups are about a year old, they are active participants in the kill, although still a little inept and reliant upon the more experienced adults.

Wolves have developed a practical hunting tactic for use against high country prey. In hunting Dall's sheep in Alaska, and both bighorn sheep and mountain goats in the Canadian Rockies, they use an over-the-top strategy that eliminates the prey's primary defense: height. The pack climbs a mountain or ridge on the side opposite their prey, crests the summit, and charges down on their victims, literally out of the blue. Surprisingly, wolves use this tactic in the winter, plowing their way up through deep mountain snows and then descending like an avalanche of fangs on their prey. If they've done everything right (they often don't) the prey will have nowhere to go but down, farther and farther from the safety of cliffs. More often than not, the intended prey manages to sprint laterally across the slope and onto cliffs and narrow ledges where the wolves cannot follow.

Most theories on behavioral biology would predict that wolves would not hunt like this. Predator-prey relationships are thought to be based on pretty much one thing: calories. Or more specifically, predators acquiring them. This idea is strongly linked to a gen-

eral biological concept called *optimality theory*. Basically, optimality theory holds that predators should hunt in a way that maximizes their caloric intake while minimizing their effort, or calories expended. Makes sense—take what's easiest to kill and fill your belly. For many predators this holds true, but not for wolves. A select group of predators—notably chimps, humans, a few species of whale and dolphin, and wolves—have gone well beyond simple optimality theory and developed particular tastes. These could be considered cravings with no apparent biological rhyme or reason. In the Canadian Rockies, wolves living in elk- and sheep-filled valleys will set off on two-day, fifty-mile round-trip hunts to bring down and consume a single scrawny Mountain caribou. Did they just get sick of mutton? Or maybe the journey was an adventure, a road trip with a meal at the far end. In part because of situations like this, optimality theory is no longer used to predict animal behavior outside of a petri dish. Rather, it is now most often used to establish a sort of theoretical baseline to which real behaviors can be compared and referenced.

Packs stake out territories of anywhere from twenty to well over six hundred square miles, regularly patrolling boundaries and marking predominant objects along their borders, such as stumps, trees, and rocks, with urine. These marked objects, called scent posts, act as "keep out" signs to neighboring packs. Even packs in hot pursuit of wounded prey often will not cross these borders; their hunger and desperation must be extreme before they will risk violating another pack's turf.

Both pack size and territory size seem to be tied to the abundance of prey and to how many breeding-age adults are in the group. Large packs with several

WOLVES, OVER-THE-TOP HUNTING, NORTHWEST MONTANA

breeding-age pairs in game-poor territories are likely to have many internal conflicts over food, mates, and rank. The social pressure, combined with the empty stomachs, keeps aggression high and these packs are likely to fragment. Sometimes the fragmentation is complete with wars, shifting borders and alliances, and even defections as the original pack's large territory is divided up into smaller parcels.

The break-up of a pack can have wide-ranging repercussions. As the pack fragments, individuals and pairs take off in all directions, sometimes wandering dozens of miles a day. Often they are pioneers, exploring vast new regions containing only faint sign of their own kind. It is these pioneers that are slowly recolonizing the Rockies of the U.S.; a few reached as far south as Yellowstone before wolves were transplanted there from Canada.

Wolves are currently hunted where they are relatively plentiful: throughout most of western Canada and in parts of Alaska. In the lower forty-eight, they are listed as threatened in Minnesota and endangered elsewhere. Ironically, it is this protected status that is hindering some reintroduction efforts. Ranchers and herders fear having their hands tied by federal regulations in the face of depredations against their stock. And their fears are real and deeply felt. These people devote a tremendous amount of time and effort to raising their stock: eighteen-hour work days, carrying newborn calves into barns during blizzards, and seemingly endless tending to the general welfare of their herds. Seeing a favorite old breeding cow that has been torn-up by wolves is as heart-wrenching as if the victim were a family pet. And it does occasion-

ally happen. Some wolves deviate from their normal diets of wild game and develop a taste for livestock. Fortunately, such wolves are rare (if they were common, there wouldn't be a cow standing in northern Minnesota). Only when we provide livestock owners with the ability to protect their herds against the occasional marauder will wolves generally be accepted as a part of the American West. Then we will finally hear their songs echoing among the mountains.

Coyote

The coyote is arguably the most versatile, durable predator walking the earth today. After decades of relentless persecution by humans, coyotes have not only managed to expand their range, but have also actually altered their behavior so fundamentally that they literally now live in the shadow of man. Ranging from Mexico to Alaska and coast to coast, coyotes have successfully occupied every type of North American environment: swamps, deserts, mountains, prairie, and even urban areas. In recent years, they have even expanded their range into the industrialized northeastern United States.

Although some have been reported to be as large as forty-five pounds, coyotes typically weigh between eighteen and thirty pounds. Their long legs and bushy coats give them a considerably larger appearance; at a distance, a typical twenty-five—pounder looks almost as large and heavy as a sixty-pound German shepherd. Larger coyotes are often mistaken for wolves, but there are some very distinct physical differences between the two. The coyote's head in relation to its body is proportionately much smaller and more delicate looking than a wolf's. Also, the coyote's bushier fur coat makes it look like a bottlebrush with legs,

whereas a wolf has a deep chest and a well-defined waist. Coyotes tend to trot with tail and heads held low, whereas wolves tend to hold their tails in the same axis as their bodies with their heads higher. Coyotes have long, very thin legs with tiny feet under three inches in diameter, whereas wolves have long, sturdy legs with large feet up to six inches in diameter.

The majority of the coyote's diet, sixty percent or more, is made up of rabbits, hares, and rodents. In the high country they pursue marmots, pika, ground squirrels, and ptarmigan. The rest is primarily carrion, although sometimes they hunt infirm or newborn ungulates such as deer and elk fawns and bighorn lambs. On occasion, sizable numbers of coyotes get together to take down larger game animals such as elk, but these temporary gangs have virtually no social structure. They are packs that form on the spot near an injured or frail prey animal. The first coyotes on the scene, realizing they can't take the animal down, begin howling, and soon a hungry crowd gathers. Snapping and yapping, they swarm over their prey, killing it, bolting down food as quickly as possible, and carrying off as much as they can. In a matter of hours, even an animal as large as an elk is reduced to a few bones and scraps of hide. The pack dissolves and all the individuals and pairs head home to their territories, dens, mates, or pups.

Coyotes typically breed in February, have an approximately sixty-day gestation period, and the average litter size is between five and seven. Litters of a dozen or more aren't uncommon and at least one of nineteen has been reported (although this may have been pups from two different mothers living in the same den). Depending on the season, the usual social unit is a mated pair and possibly their pups. The pair will stake out an exclusive territory of five or more acres around their den, which is usually a burrow, and hunts through a larger home range of five to twenty-five square miles. They raise their pups cooperatively, moving them to a rendezvous area or a new den when they are two to four months old. The male will bring food to the female, and later to the pups, regurgitating on demand as wolves do. Even after the pups are weaned and both adults are out hunting, the female will occasionally solicit a meal for herself from the male.

Where wolf social life revolves around the pack, community living is an option for coyotes. Sometimes, all through mating, denning, and raising the pups, an extra female hangs around with the mated pair. She is usually the mother's sister or a daughter from the previous year, and she helps in feeding and baby-sitting the pups. Sometimes other individuals show up, both male and female, and they too help in raising the pups. They may stick around for a few days, or a few months. What's interesting about this is that the mated pair won't let just anyone approach their den. Some individuals are driven off immediately, while others are accepted just as quickly. In other species where helpers work with the parents to raise the young, such as hyenas and some birds, the helpers are almost always brothers and sisters of the parents and young from a previous year. This is also the case with coyotes. When relatives help out, they are actually enhancing their own genetic fitness. Since they share so many common genes with the young they are helping to raise, they are nurturing their own genes and helping them to pass into the future. It's a sort of surrogate reproduction that allows non-breeding individuals to insure their own genetic success. Overall, coyotes are not pack animals, but when the need for assistance arises, such as feeding pups or taking down big game, they will band together and form a loosely structured pack to help each other out.

Grizzly

No individual animal dominates its surrounding environment like the grizzly bear. At up to twelve hundred pounds, it is the largest carnivore walking the earth and can take down any North American animal it chooses. Despite its roly-poly looks, it is explosively quick and powerful, able to accelerate from zero to thirty miles per hour faster than most high-performance sports cars. Its toughness and resilience when injured are legendary, as is its temper. Lewis and Clark reported an incident in which a plains grizzly in eastern Montana not only survived hits by over a dozen .45 and .50 caliber rifle rounds, but went on the offensive and attacked its assailants. It reportedly took nearly twenty rounds to kill the animal.

Grizzlies are armed with four-inch-plus claws on all four feet and jaws capable of shearing through a moose thigh bone with one bite. Thanks to the huge hump of muscle on their shoulders, their forelimbs are enormously powerful. One swat from a forepaw is enough to bring down all but the largest prey. Yet despite this arsenal, these massive carnivores are primarily vegetarians. They live out most of their lives peacefully digging up roots and grazing on fresh greens and ripening berries. It is only when the craving for meat takes them, or when confronted by danger to themselves or their young, that the deadly predator in them comes alive. And then they are truly awesome.

Grizzlies are not truly territorial, but rather, they roam through a home range of up to a thousand square miles. Each bear carries with it a sort of portable mini-territory, a personal space around itself that it will defend vigorously against any intruder.

GRIZZLY BEAR, BANFF NATIONAL PARK

The mood or individual disposition of the bear defines the size of this space. It may be only a couple hundred feet or several hundred yards in diameter; it is this unpredictable possessiveness that gets most humans into trouble with the great bear.

Basically, if you're close enough to get a good look at a grizzly, even with binoculars, you're probably too close; a grizzly can cover a quarter of a mile faster than a human can run a hundred yards over broken terrain. And if the bear charges you, it has probably judged that it can catch you and is almost certainly right.

Human survivors of grizzly attacks all describe the same things: overwhelming speed and power. Brush cracking as if a derailed train were bearing down on them, deafening roars, and then boom! Restraint. Not death and blackness as the bear exerts a tiny fraction of its enormous power and crushes the skull or pulverizes the spine, but restraint. A rebuff. A few bone-cracking casual swats, a couple of lung-piercing nips and the bear leaves. A few attacks are fatal, and a few people actually get eaten, but the restraint exercised by the bear is what stands out in most attacks. These animals could easily pound a human being into an unrecognizable mass, yet their attacks most often resemble a bear-to-bear chastisement. We seem to be viewed as competitors to be kept away from cubs or driven out of a favored berry patch or away from some nice, juicy carrion. In short, we're a nuisance.

Unlike marmots and ground squirrels, grizzlies are not true hibernators. What they do in their dens through the winter is best described as a deep sleep. Their body temperature, heart and respiration rates all fall slightly lower than in a normal sleep, but they do not descend to anywhere near the dead-to-the-world state of the squirrels. Grizzlies frequently awaken during the winter, sometimes due to disturbances, or just to change positions. Some go out and wander around for days, or even weeks, snacking on carrion or leftover, frozen berries.

Most interesting, though, is that it is during this deep winter sleep that birth occurs. Grizzlies typically mate in June and July, and like weasels, have delayed implantation. Embryonic development delays for at least three months, until the female, called a sow, settles in to sleep sometime in November. She sleeps through most of her pregnancy, and may even sleep through the birth itself, which occurs in January or February. Imagine the quiet darkness, winter raging outside. Up to four, one-pound, naked, blind cubs whimper and squirm their way across their mother's enormous body to her bosom to suckle. For the next three months, locked under the snow, the cubs will hardly move from their mother's breast. The whole family survives solely on her fat reserves.

The cubs gain up to ten pounds before the family emerges from the den in March or April. Immediately upon leaving the den, they begin living on the move, roaming through the sow's home range. The sow grazes on succulent spring growth, or, if she's lucky she may find carrion or easy prey. She stops frequently to let her cubs nurse and to play with them. During this first summer the cubs' lives are free and easy, with frolicsome mornings and lazy warm afternoons. The burden of worry falls on the sow, and she is fiercely protective and constantly alert, especially for boars, her male counterpart. Male grizzlies, particularly older, larger individuals, tend to kill and eat unguarded cubs. The sow's fearless aggression in the presence of a male is unparalleled. One moment she will be quietly nursing and coddling her cubs and the next she has exploded into a foaming, demonic rage

Grizzly bear digging roots, Glacier National Park

and is bearing down on a male twice her size. Even with his overwhelming physical superiority, the intruding boar usually backs down, recognizing that while he may eventually prevail, there is no way he will avoid tremendous damage from the sow. A couple of meals usually aren't worth it.

While they are long lived (many wild bears have been aged into their late twenties), grizzlies are not very productive animals. Females typically do not mate until they are over three years old, and in some particularly harsh environments, not until they are five or older. Once a female does begin to breed, she will probably mate only once every three years and will normally have two cubs in each litter. Depending on the region, cub mortality ranges from twenty to eighty percent, and adult sow mortality can push twenty-five percent, much of this caused by boars. In the open tundra of the far north and the high country, animal fat and protein are hard to come by and in such trying environments, sows and cubs are often viewed as prey by the larger, more aggressive boars.

Unlike a typical black bear family, which stays together for only one season, grizzly families stay together for two years, sometimes even three. By the end of their first summer, the cubs can weigh over a hundred pounds and will be eating an adult diet, although their mother will still let them nurse occasionally. The family dens together through the winter, sometimes in the same den where the cubs were born. During this time, the bears lose up to a third of their body weight. This is a major setback for the growing cubs, the first of many in the two-steps-forward, one-step-back life of a typical bear. From this point on, the cubs will always be racing the clock, constantly eating, gathering the reserves that will

allow them not only to survive their winter sleep, but also to grow.

Their second summer will not be nearly so carefree as their first. Constantly ravenous, they can't rely on their mother anymore for food. Before, playing and sleeping dominated their lives; now eating, endless eating, and growing do. Having emerged from their winter sleep as light as fifty to seventy-five pounds, by the end of their second summer they are topping two hundred. And now the family is something else altogether. They are a pack of grizzlies, up to four strong, and if you are a prey animal you'd better be healthy and fast, or you're dinner.

As formidable as this group sounds, it is far from invincible. In Denali National Park, Alaska, two of nature's titans, a wolf pack and a grizzly family, met in a violent, bloody confrontation—a confrontation that resulted in the grizzlies, the high country's most powerful individual predators, becoming prey. A sow grizzly and her three yearling cubs were foraging on Sable Pass when a pack of eleven or twelve wolves suddenly appeared over a rise and bore down on them. The sow immediately sensed that this was serious and began to retreat with her cubs. The pack pressed in, easily overtaking the bears and surrounding them. Even with their enormous combined power, the bears were no match for the speed and coordination of the wolf pack. The grizzlies' swats raked only air while the wolves zipped in and out, ripping at flanks and hindquarters. In a matter of minutes, the wolves managed to separate two of the cubs from the sow. Against these overwhelming odds, the sow had no choice but to continue her retreat with her remaining cub. The pack fell on the two cubs and they lasted only moments. Within a few hours all that remained of the cubs were bits of hair scattered across the tundra.

Grizzlies once roamed the mountains of northern Mexico, north throughout most of the U.S. west of the Mississippi and up through Canada and Alaska. In the lower forty-eight alone, there were probably more than fifty thousand of them with some estimates pushing one hundred thousand. Today, south of the Canadian border, there are probably no more than eight hundred grizzlies roaming over about one percent of their former range. While a few are rumored to exist in small holdouts in Mexico and Colorado, grizzly country really starts in the Yellowstone region of northern Wyoming and runs north through eastern Idaho and western Montana. As many as thirty-five thousand grizzlies range throughout British Columbia, western Alberta, Yukon, the Northwest territories, and Alaska.

North America's grizzlies were once split up into over a dozen subspecies and considered separate from European brown bears. Recently, all grizzlies, including European bears, have been reclassified as *Ursus arctos*, and only a few subspecies are recognized. This new classification will undoubtedly change in the next decade or so as advanced genetic testing answers once and for all, "Who's related to whom?"

Grizzlies regularly wander the high country, particularly in the mountain spring, June and early July, and then again in the fall. They follow the spring, from lower to higher altitudes as the snow melts its way up the mountains. By doing this, they are able to feed on the freshest, most nutritious greens well into the summer. They also spend a lot of time in and around avalanche chutes searching for victims of winter slides and eating greenery off low-lying vegetation common to these areas. Later in the season, when berries begin to ripen, they descend below tree line to take advantage of this rich, sugary crop. After

the berries pass their peak, the bears head back up the mountains to dig up roots and ground squirrels, both of which are at their peaks as food sources. The roots are loaded with the stored starches that provide the energy the plant needs to bloom the following spring, and the ground squirrels are at their fattest as they prepare for hibernation. Places where the bears have been digging look like they've been rototilled. These areas, and the huge pits they excavate to get to ground squirrel dens, are called digs. Aside from a direct encounter, nothing can make you tingle like coming across a fresh, steaming dig at dawn in the mountains, complete with enormous crumbling footprints in the freshly churned earth—you instantly consider your place on the food chain.

THRONE AND BLACKHORN MOUNTAINS AND AMETHYST RIVER, JASPER NATIONAL PARK

FINAL
THOUGHTS

FINAL THOUGHTS

Genetic information in the form of living individuals, species, and the dynamic, interacting communities they create, is a resource vastly more valuable than coal or oil. It is the resource that defines the very character of life on this planet. Every plant or animal that we consume—virtually every antibiotic, every fiber, even the air that we breath—was not initially engineered in a computer: The natural world provided them to us in their basic forms. All were produced by a world bursting with species and their endless combinations of competition, predation, diseases, successes, failures, disasters, and opportunities.

Australopithecus, Neanderthal, Peking, and Piltdown are all extinct creatures. Yet bits and pieces of them are sitting here reading this book. How can this be? How can you exist if your ancestors all went extinct? Simple: They weren't annihilated. They evolved, a select few surviving and dominating, adapting to a changing world, passing a little of themselves into the future. After the fact, we look back in the fossil record and we say that the earlier forms of plants and animals have gone extinct. Often, they went extinct only in the sense that they have changed into something else, a new species. We are living proof that nature frequently leaves something behind—somehow, in some way, enough tough, resilient individuals survive to carry their species' genetic legacy into the future. These individuals are the seeds of new species, their genes the building blocks of future life.

But human-caused extinctions usually have nothing to do with evolution. When we cause extinctions, no individuals or genetic seeds are left behind. Methodically, and with frightening speed, we are mowing down species after species, robbing the future of their genes and the life forms they would have become. But we are not only destroying species, we are also meddling with the very forces of creation: meddling in ways that may have dire consequences for our own species. Our kind of extinction is forever, and it leaves an empty void. Have we already sealed our own fate by slashing and burning the cure to some future plague? How is it that so many endangered rain forest amphibians are virtually invincible to viral attacks? Are today's tropical amphibians descendants of the survivors of ancient viral epidemics? Will we find out before they are gone? As we sit here now, is some primate fighting an evolutionary battle with the HIV virus and winning? We can't simply duplicate this process with a

Above: Hoary marmot, Mount Rainier National Park, Washington

Opposite: Swiftcurrent Peak, Glacier National Park

few chimps in a lab; it could easily take vast populations ranging across a variety of environments to find the unique combination of genetic and environmental factors that lead to victory.

Living, interacting wild communities are fighting and winning battles every day and we benefit from their struggles. Penicillin fought and conquered bacterial competitors long before it was discovered by man—Alexander Fleming just happened to find the winner and now it fights our bacterial competitors. Vast communities of plants, insects, animals, and microorganisms are duking it out for survival every second of every day, and every winner of every battle carries in its genes an answer. An answer that we may need one day.

All of the creatures of *High Life* are not only living solutions to the problems of ice-age survival, but are also solutions in the making. They are adapting to a continually changing world and will find answers to future problems, problems that we too will face. When the inevitable climatic shifts of the future occur, where will we turn for the knowledge and genetic stocks needed to survive in a new world? As always, we will turn to the plants and animals of the natural world. They've been there.

MOON OVER RUNNING RABBIT MOUNTAIN, GLACIER NATIONAL PARK

Selected Bibliography

A WORLD OF ICE

Flint, Richard Foster. *Glacial Geology and the Pleistocene Epoch.* New York: Wiley and Sons, 1967.

Gadd, Ben. *The Handbook of the Canadian Rockies.* Jasper, Alberta: Corax Press, 1995.

Hopkins, David. *The Bering Land Bridge.* Stanford, CA: Stanford University Press, 1967.

Levin, Harold. *The Earth Through Time.* Philadelphia: W.B. Sanders Co., 1978.

Strickler, Dee. *Alpine Wildflowers.* Kalamazoo, MI: The Flower Press, 1990.

Time-Life Editors. *Grasslands and Tundra.* Alexandria, VA: Time-Life Books, 1985.

Zwinger, Ann, and Beatrice Willard. *Land Above the Trees.* Tucson: University of Arizona Press, 1972.

THE ROCKPILE COMMUNITY

Armitage, Kenneth. "Social Behavior of a Colony of the Yellow-bellied Marmot (*Marmota flaviventris*)." *Animal Behavior* 10 (1962): 319–331.

Barash, D.P. "Habitat Utilization in Three Species of Subalpine Mammals." *Journal of Mammalogy* 54, no. 1 (1973): 247–250.

Barash, D.P. "The Evolution of Marmot Societies: a General Theory." *Science* 185 (1974): 415–420.

Barash, D.P. "Territorial and Foraging Behavior of Pika in Montana." *American Midland Naturalist* 89, no. 1 (1973): 202–207.

Brody, Alison, and Jaye Melcher. "Maternal Care and Behavioral Development in Pikas (*Ochotona princeps*)." *Animal Behavior* 32 (1984): 743–752.

Brody, Alison, and Jaye Melcher. "Infanticide in Yellow-bellied Marmots (*Marmota flaviventris*)." *Animal Behavior* 33 (1985): 673–674.

Brown, Richard N., Charles H. Southwick, and Steven C. Golian. "Male-Female Spacing, Territorial Replacement and the Mating System of Pikas (*Ochotona princeps*)." *Journal of Mammalogy* 70 (1989): 622–627.

Hoffman, R.F., and C.F. Nadler. "Chromosomes and Systematics of some North American Species of the Genus Marmota." *Experientia* 24 (1968): 740–742.

Murie, Jan, and Gail Michener, eds. *The Biology of Ground-Dwelling Squirrels.* Lincoln: University of Nebraska Press, 1984.

Tolliver, T, M. H. Smith, P. Jones, and M.W. Smith. "Low Levels of Genetic Variability in Pikas from Colorado." *Canadian Journal of Zoology.* July 1985: 1735–1737.

Tyser, Robin W. "Foraging and Substrate Use Patterns in Talus Slope Mammals." Ph.D. diss., University of Wisconsin, Madison, 1978.

Waterman, Jane. "Infanticide in the Columbian Ground Squirrel (*Spermophilus columbianus*)." *Journal of Mammalogy* 65 (1984): 137–138.

Wright, Phillip. "Montana's Alpine Whistler." *Montana Outdoors* 21, no. 2 (1990): 32–34.

THE FEATHERED COMMUNITY

Arnold, Lee. *The Golden Eagle and Its Economic Status.* U.S. Fish and Wildlife, 1954.

Ashley, John. *Progress Report: Harlequin Duck Inventory and Monitoring in Glacier National Park, Montana.* Glacier National Park Report, 1994.

Braun, Clait. "The White-tailed Ptarmigan in Colorado." State of Colorado, Publication #27.

Chadwick, Doug. "The Harlequin Duck: Bird of White Waters." *National Geographic.* November 1993: 116–132.

Choate, Thomas. *Reproduction and Turnover in an Unhunted White-tail Ptarmigan Population.* Transaction of the 6th Congress of the International Union of Game Biologists, London, 1963.

Choate, Thomas. "Habitat and Population Dynamics of White-tail Ptarmigan in Montana." *Journal of*

Wildlife Management 27 (1963): 684–699.

Clarkson, Peter. *A Preliminary Investigation into the Status and Distribution of Harlequin Ducks in Jasper National Park.* Warden Service, Jasper, Canada, 1992.

Dorst, Jean. *The Life of Birds.* New York: Columbia University Press, 1974.

Ehrlich, Paul R., David S. Dobkin, and Darryl Wheye. *The Birder's Handbook.* New York: Simon and Schuster, 1988.

Johnson, Richard. "Temperature Regulation in the White-tailed Ptarmigan (*Lagopus leucerus*)." M.S. diss., University of Montana, Missoula, 1968.

Kuchel, Craig. *Some Aspects of the Behavioral Biology and Ecology of Harlequin Ducks Breeding in Glacier National Park, Montana.* Master's thesis, Missoula: University on Montana, 1977.

McGahan, Jerry. "Ecology of the Golden Eagle." *The Auk* 85 (1968): 1–12.

Nietfield, Linda. "Daring Dippers." *Ranger Rick.* March 1993: 28–30.

"Pee in the U.V." *Discover.* May 1995: 17.

THE HOOFED COMMUNITY

Brown, W.K., and J.L. Kansas. *The Greater Jasper Ecosystem Caribou Research Project.* Calgary, Alberta, Canada: Sentar Consultants, 1994.

Chadwick, Doug. *A Beast the Color of Winter.* San Francisco: Sierra Club Books, 1983.

Chadwick, Doug. *Ecology of the Rocky Mountain Goat in Glacier National Park, Montana.* Glacier National Park Report, 1977.

Demarchi, Raymond. "Chemical Composition of Bighorn Winter Forages." *Journal of Range Management* 21, no. 9 (1968): 385–388.

Evans, H.F. *A Preliminary Investigation of Caribou in the Northwestern United States.* Master's thesis, Bozeman: Montana State University, 1960.

Geist, Valerius. *Mountain Sheep.* University of Chicago Press, 1971.

Geist, Valerius. *Mountain Sheep and Man.* Cornell University Press, 1975.

Geist, Valerius. *Wild Sheep Country.* Minocqua, WI: NorthWord Press, 1993.

Harrington , C.R. "A Pleistocene Mountain Goat from British Columbia and Comments on the Dispersal of *Oreamnus*." *Canadian Journal of Earth Sciences* 8, no. 9 (1971): 1081–1093.

Hibbs, L.D. *A Literature Review of Mountain Goat Ecology.* State of Colorado Publication. Special Report #8. July 1966.

Keating, Kim. *Evaluating the Natural Status of Bighorn Sheep Epizootics in Glacier National Park, Montana.* Glacier National Park Report, 1985.

Korobitsyna, K. V., C. F. Nadler, and N. N. Vorontsov. "Chromosomes of the Siberian Snow Sheep (*Ovis nivicola*), and Implications Concerning the Origins of Amphiberingian Wild Sheep." *Quaternary Research* 4 (1974): 235–245.

Kurten, Bjorn, and Elaine Anderson. *Pleistocene Mammals of North America.* New York: Columbia University Press, 1980.

Meagher, Mary, William J. Quinn, and Larry Stackhouse. "Chlamydial-caused Infectious Keratoconjuntivitis in Bighorn Sheep of Yellowstone National Park." *Journal of Wildlife Diseases* 28, no. 2 (1992): 171–176.

Miller, Don. *The Feasibility of Reintroducing Caribou in Glacier National Park; a Preliminary Study.* Glacier National Park Report, 1976.

Stevens, David R., and Donay D. Hanson. *The Use of Transplanting to Expand Bighorn Sheep Range.* Procedings from the 5th Symposium of the Northern Wild Sheep and Goat Council, April, 1986.

Thorne, E. T., N. Kingston, W. R. Jolley, and R. C. Bergstrom. Diseases of *Wildlife in Wyoming.* Wyoming Game and Fish Department, 1982.

THE THREAT FROM BELOW

Banci, Vivian. *American Marten, Fisher, Lynx, and Wolverine in the United States.* USDA Technical Report RM-254. September 1994: 99–127.

Brown Bear Resources Editors. *Silvertip Tracks* 3, no. 2 (1995), whole issue.

Boyd, Diane, and Michael Jimenez. "Successful Rearing of Young by Wild Wolves Without Mates." *Journal of Mammalogy* 75, no. 1 (1994): 14–17.

Craighead, F. Jr. *Track of the Grizzly.* San Francisco: Sierra Club Books, 1979.

Curnow, Edward. "The History of the Eradication of the Wolf in Montana." M.A. Thesis, University of Montana, Missoula, 1969.

Day, Gary. "The Status and Distibution of Wolves in the Northern Rocky Mountains of the United States." M.S. Diss., University of Montana, Missoula, 1981.

Harrington, Fred H., and Paul C. Paquet. *Wolves of the World: Perspectives of Behavior, Ecology, and Conservation.* Park Ridge, NJ: Noyes Publications, 1982.

Hornocker, Mauriece G., and Howard S. Hash. "Ecology of the Wolverine in Northwestern Montana." *Canadian Journal of Zoology* 59, no. 7 (1981): 1286–1301.

Koehler, Gary M., Mauriece G. Hornocker, and Howard S. Hash. "Wolverine Marking Behavior." *Canadian Field Naturalist* 94 (1980): 339–341.

Murie, Adolph. *The Ecology of the Coyote in Yellowstone.* U.S. Government Printing Office, 1940.

Parnell, Michael. "Lions on the Prowl." *Colorado Outdoors* 38, no. 6 (1989): 8–10.

Robinson, David. *Puma! Puma!* Las Vegas: Defenders Publications. 1976.

Russel, A. *Grizzly Country.* New York: Alfred A. Knopf, 1968.

Ryden, Hope. God's Dog: *The North American Coyote.* New York: Lyons and Burford, 1979.

Savage, Candace. *Wolves.* San Francisco: Sierra Club Books, 1988.

Seidensticker, John C. IV, Mauriece G. Hornocker, Wilbur V. Wiles, and John P. Messick. *Mountain Lion Social Organization in the Idaho Primitive Area.* Wildlife Monographs. Vol. 35, 1973.

Young, Stanley P., and Hartley H.T. Jackson. *The Clever Coyote.* Lincoln: University of Nebraska Press, 1951.

Recommended Reading

Chadwick, Doug. *A Beast the Color of Winter.* San Francisco: Sierra Club Books, 1983.

Gadd, Ben. *The Handbook of the Canadian Rockies.* Jasper, Alberta: Corax Press, 1995.

Geist, Valerius. *Wild Sheep Country.* Minocqua, WI: NorthWord Press, 1993.

Zwinger, Ann and Willard, Beatrice. *Land Above the Trees.* Tucson: University of Arizona Press, 1972.

Index

Page numbers in *italics* refer to photographs.

About the Author

John Winnie, Jr., grew up with a fascination for wildlife and wild places. He carried this interest with him to the University of Montana, where he received his degree in Zoology. He earned money for school by working in Glacier National Park, Montana, and it was there that his passion for nature photography was born. In the years since, he has traveled and photographed extensively throughout the mountains of the western United States and Canada, from Alaska and the Yukon Territory south through the Rocky Mountains.

John's photography has appeared in *American Birds, Montana Magazine, Montana Outdoors,* and *Whitefish Magazine,* and numerous local, regional, and national advertisements, as well as posters, calendars, and postcards. He was also co-photographer for *The Rockies: Canada's Magnificent Wilderness,* published by Beautiful America Publishing in 1992.